Access to History: In Depth

General Editor: Robert Pearce

Spain in the Reigns of Isabella and Ferdinand, 1474-1516

Geoffrey Woodward

Hodder & Stoughton

A MEMBER OF THE HODDER HEADLINE

The cover illustration is a painting of Queeen Isabella and King Ferdinand
(courtesy of Topham Picture Point)

Order: Please contact Bookpoint Ltd, 130 Milton Park, Abingdon,
Oxon OX14 4SB. Telephone: (44) 01235 400414.
Fax: (44) 01235 400454. Lines are open from 9 am – 6 pm
Monday to Saturday, with a 24-hour message answering service.
Email address: orders@bookpoint.co.uk

British Library Cataloguing in Publication Data
A catalogue record for this title is available from The British Library

ISBN 0 340 68852 1

First published 1997
Impression number   12 11 10 9 8 7 6 5
Year   2004 2003 2002 2001

Typeset by Sempringham Publishing, Bedford.
Printed in Great Britain for Hodder & Stoughton Educational,
a division of Hodder Headline Plc, 338, Euston Road, London NW1 3BH
by The Bath Press, Bath

Contents

Acknowledgements

The publishers would like to thank the following for permission to reproduce the following copyright illustrations:

Cover - a painting of Queen Isabella and King Ferdinand (courtesy of Topham Picture Point). Page 22, courtesy of the Spanish Tourist Office, London; pages 81 and 95, Mary Evans Picture Library, London.

The publishers would like to thank the following for permission to reproduce material in this volume:

Blackwell for extracts from *Spain 1516-1598: From Nation State to World Empire* by John Lynch (1991) and 'Henry VII and the Treaty of Redon (1489): Plantagenet Ambitions and Early Tudor Foreign Policy' in *History*, vol. 81 by John M. Currin (1996); Boydell and Brewer Ltd for an extract from *Money, Prices and Politics in Fifteenth-Century Castile* by Angus Mackay (1981); Cambridge University Press for extracts from *Christian Córdoba* by John Edwards (1982) and *Keepers of the City* by Marvin Lunenfeld (1987); Oxford University Press for extracts from *The Medieval Crown of Aragon* by T.N. Bisson (1986), *The Spanish Kingdoms, 1410-1516*, vol. 2 by J.N. Hillgarth (1978) and *The European Dynastic States, 1494-1660* by Richard Bonney (1991); Hambledon Press for extracts from 'National Consciousness in Early Modern Spain' in *Politicians and Virtuosi: Essays in Early Modern History* by Helmut Koenigsberger (1986); Medieval Academy of America for an extract from *Enrique IV and the Crisis of Fifteenth Century Castile 1425-1480* by W.D. Phillips (1978); Penguin Books Ltd for extracts from *The Prince* by Machiavelli (ed. G. Bull) (1981) and *Renaissance Diplomacy* by Garrett Mattingley (1965); Peters Fraser and Dunlop Group Ltd for extracts from *Spain 1469-1714: A Society in Conflict* by Henry Kamen (Longman, 1991); Routledge for extracts from *The Age of Discovery, 1400-1600* by David Arnold (1983); Weidenfeld and Nicolson for extracts from *Inquisition and Society in Spain* by Henry Kamen (1985).

Every effort has been made to trace and acknowledge ownership of copyright. The publishers will be glad to make any suitable arrangements with copyright holders whom it has not been possible to contact.

Preface

The original *Access to History* series was conceived as a collection of sets of books covering popular chronological periods in British history, such as 'The Tudors' and 'the nineteenth century', together with the histories of other countries, such as France, Germany, Russia and the USA. This arrangement complemented the way in which early-modern and modern history has traditionally been taught in sixth forms, colleges and universities. In recent years, however, other ways of dividing up the past have become increasingly popular. In particular, there has been a greater emphasis on studying relatively brief periods in considerable detail and on comparing similar historical phenomena in different countries. These developments have generated a demand for appropriate learning materials, and, in response, two new 'strands' are being added to the main series - *In Depth* and *Themes*. The new volumes build directly on the features that have made *Access to History* so popular.

To the general reader

Although *Access* books have been specifically designed to meet the needs of examination students, these volumes also have much to offer the general reader. *Access* authors are committed to the belief that good history must not only be accurate, up-to-date and scholarly, but must also be clearly and attractively written. The main body of the text (excluding the Study Guides) should, therefore, form a readable and engaging survey of a topic. Moreover, each author has aimed not merely to provide as clear an explanation as possible of what happened in the past but also to stimulate readers and to challenge them into thinking for themselves about the past and its significance. Thus, although no prior knowledge is expected from the reader, he or she is treated as an intelligent and thinking person throughout. The author tends to share ideas and explore possibilities, instead of delivering so-called 'historical truths' from on high.

To the student reader

It is intended that *Access* books should be used by students studying history at a higher level. Its volumes are all designed to be working texts, which should be reasonably clear on a first reading but which will benefit from re-reading and close study.

To be an effective and successful student, you need to budget your time wisely. Hence you should think carefully about how important the material in a particular book is for you. If you simply need to acquire a general grasp of a topic, the following approach will probably be effective:

1 Read Chapter 1, which should give you an overview of the whole book, and think about its contents.
2 Skim through Chapter 2, paying particular attention to the opening section and to the headings and sub-headings. Decide if you need to read the whole chapter.
3 If you do, read the chapter, stopping at the end of every sub-division of the text to make notes.
4 Repeat stage 2 (and stage 3 where appropriate) for the other chapters.

If, however, your course - and your particular approach to it - demands a detailed knowledge of the contents of the book, you will need to be correspondingly more thorough. There is no perfect way of studying, and it is particularly worthwhile experimenting with different styles of note-making to find the one that best suits you. Nevertheless the following plan of action is worth trying:

1 Read a whole chapter quickly, preferably at one sitting. Avoid the temptation - which may be very great - to make notes at this stage.
2 Study the flow diagram at the end of the chapter, ensuring that you understand the general 'shape' of what you have read.
3 Re-read the chapter more slowly, this time taking notes. You may well be amazed at how much more intelligible and straightforward the material seems on a second reading - and your notes will be correspondingly more useful to you when you have to write an essay or revise for an exam. In the long run, reading a chapter twice can, in fact, often save time. Be sure to make your notes in a clear, orderly fashion, and spread them out so that, if necessary, you can later add extra information.
4 Read the advice on essay questions, and do tackle the specimen titles. (Remember that if learning is to be effective, it must be active. No one - alas - has yet devised any substitute for real effort. It is up to you to make up your own mind on the key issues in any topic.)
5 Attempt the source-based questions. The guidance on tackling these exercises, which is generally given at least once in a book, is well worth reading and thinking about.

When you have finished the main chapters, go through the 'Further Reading' section. Remember that no single book can ever do more than introduce a topic, and it is to be hoped that - time permitting - you will want to read more widely. If *Access* books help you to discover just how diverse and fascinating the human past can be the series will have succeeded in its aim - and you will experience that enthusiasm for the subject which, along with efficient learning, is the hallmark of all the best students.

Robert Pearce

CHAPTER 1

The Hispanic Kingdoms in 1469

1 Introduction

This book is a study of the Hispanic kingdoms at the end of the fifteenth and beginning of the sixteenth centuries. Two main themes dominate this study: the manner in which Isabella and Ferdinand tackled their problems and how far they overcame them; and the extent to which they created a unified and united country. Each of these issues has been the subject of controversy in recent years partly because historians have disagreed over their definition of concepts such as 'country' and 'unity', and over their interpretation of continuity and change, and success and failure. In reading this book, you should consistently ask why historians argue, which lines of argument appear the most acceptable and which interpretations should remain provisional. The first chapter outlines the geographical and political conditions in the peninsula before turning to social, economic, religious, cultural and foreign affairs in 1469.

The Iberian peninsula comprised the kingdoms of Castile, Aragon, Catalonia, Valencia, Navarre, Portugal and the emirate of Granada (see map on page 2). Castile had been ruled by the Trastámara family since 1369 and was the largest and richest kingdom. In 1469 its king was Henry IV (1454-74). The Crown of Aragon comprised Aragon, Catalonia and Valencia and was ruled by John II (1458-79). He too was a Trastámara but relations between the two families were at best cool and at times hostile. Navarre straddled the Pyrenees and, although it was an independent kingdom, both French and Aragonese noble families had claims to it and the King of Castile was acknowledged as its overlord. Its unique Basque language and isolated communities largely explained its individuality. To the south of the peninsula lay Granada, a Muslim province, outside the pale of Hispanic rulers, although its emirs paid an annual tribute to Castile as a token of good will. Border relations were far from stable even though the frontier itself had moved very little since the thirteenth century. Portugal constituted a distinct kingdom with its own language, culture and institutions, and was ruled by the House of Braganza.

Occasionally, the Hispanic kingdoms will be referred to as 'Spain', although this term was not widely used within the peninsula, and even today many inhabitants of Barcelona and Navarre regard themselves as Catalonians or Basques rather than Spanish. Why this should be so will become increasingly apparent in the course of this study. Social and economic, cultural and linguistic differences within the peninsula are central issues as are the political and administrative institutions. Indeed on the face of it, the forces of regionalism and separatism were so strongly ingrained in the history and temperament of the people that applying the concept of unity or unification to the Hispanic kingdoms of the early modern period seems anachronistic. And yet is it? Contemporary chroniclers and subsequent historians have generally agreed that the reigns of Isabella of Castile (1474-1504) and Ferdinand of Aragon (1479-1516) unified Spain, gave Castilians supreme self-confidence, and laid the foundations of the Golden Age of Spain.

2 Castile

a) The Crown and its Administration

The kingdom of Castile had been ruled by Henry IV since 1454. For ten years he administered his country effectively, commanding widespread support and obedience. The Crown was potentially very strong.

The Iberian peninsula in the fifteenth century

According to a thirteenth-century law code, the *Partidas* (see Glossary for all Spanish terms), the King held power from God and was in theory above the law. Anyone who attacked or killed the King 'would be committing an attack on the kingdom itself, for one would be removing the head that Providence gave to it, and the very life by means of which the kingdom lives in unity'.[1] This belief in royal absolutism largely explains why Henry IV rejected out of hand suggestions from some of his nobles that his power could and should be limited, even though the *Partidas* also stated that laws could not be annulled 'without the advice of all the best, most honest, and wisest men of the land'.

The Castilian Cortes, the parliamentary assembly, exercised little influence over the Crown. Just 15 cities and two towns were represented by their elected delegates. They could petition the Crown about new taxes or legislation but they could not refuse or annul a law, and met only when summoned by the King. Its main function was to vote financial grants and to publish laws made by the King. If petitions were submitted, they were usually met with evasive replies from the Crown. In the early fourteenth century more than 100 towns had elected delegates to the Cortes, but by the 1460s it was a shadow of its former self. Few nobles or clergy attended, as they were exempt from direct taxation, and large areas in the north of the country were unrepresented. Yet despite its nominal weakness and the King's apparent power, it made good political sense for him to consult the Cortes and to allow regional assemblies to meet in Asturias and Galicia. There they recognised him as King 'in so far as he is lord of the land'. Much the same occurred in Vizcaya, in the Basque provinces, where he was acknowledged as little more than a feudal lord.

As there was no administrative capital and no fixed royal court, the Crown needed to consult the politically important groups - the nobility and the clergy - by inviting them to council meetings or by visiting them on their estates. The royal council was peripatetic and comprised twelve advisers traditionally drawn from the aristocracy and clergy but by the 1460s at least eight councillors were law graduates. These legal experts sat on committees which administered finance, justice and foreign affairs, while royal secretaries drew up agendas for the Council and implemented the monarch's will. Henry did not always attend these meetings but all decisions rested with him. The dispensing of justice was seen as a vital royal duty, and from time to time Henry, assisted by his judges, heard cases in person. No centralised judicial system operated and although attempts had been made to codify the law and rationalise the different royal, seigneurial, ecclesiastical and customary jurisdictions, little progress had been made. A court of appeal met in Valladolid but its authority was limited and largely confined to the north. In the provinces, justice was upheld by nobles and clergy who had their own courts and officials, and by local *hermandades* or brotherhoods who patrolled the countryside. These cavalry militia had intermittently operated as peacekeepers since the thirteenth century and had been revived by Henry to combat unruly nobles.

Most Castilian towns had magistrates and councillors. Many were appointed by the Crown as it attempted to influence urban political life but, once in office, the municipal office-holders who tended to be the local gentry and nobility resented further interference, and in practice much consultation occurred between the Crown and the council before each election. Since the fourteenth century royal governors known as *corregidores* had been sent to ensure that the King's justice and regulations governing the towns were enforced. What had begun as a temporary measure became a regular but increasingly unpopular practice in Henry's reign. Urban elites wished to retain control of their town's affairs, and in the 1460s therefore cities such as Burgos and Seville actually closed their gates to the Crown's *corregidores*.

Effective royal government depended upon using the power of the provincial aristocracy and nobility. Since the fourteenth century their authority had steadily increased at the expense of the Crown. The Luna family, for example, controlled Andalucía, and the Fajardos Murcia and the Mendozas much of New Castile. Most grandees were militarily as well as financially strong. The Marquis of Villena, for instance, held 25,000 square kilometres of land containing some 150,000 vassals, and the Masters of the three military orders controlled thousands of men in La Mancha, Extremadura, and on the frontier with Granada.

The Crown's finances were a constant source of worry, not because the potential revenue was low but because, while levels of expenditure were constantly rising, so little actually reached the Treasury.[2] The Crown's revenue in 1458 totalled 85 million *maravedis,* but currency devaluations and widespread corruption among tax collectors resulted in a steady deficit. Royal attitudes seemed indifferent to reform. The Treasury was staffed by only two chief controllers together with official receivers and collectors who were inclined to exempt taxpayers in return for bribes. As both the clergy and nobility paid no direct taxation, the Crown relied most heavily upon the *alcabala,* an indirect sales tax, and to a lesser extent on smaller sums derived from customs duties, tithes, parliamentary subsidies, and taxes on salt and sheep. In emergencies the Crown resorted to borrowing money and imposing special taxes. Henry IV was therefore as dependent upon his nobility for loans in peacetime as he was for troops in war, and to reward them it was necessary for him to divest the royal patrimony of even more estates, thereby further weakening his position. That he should find himself at war with them in the last ten years of his reign was a reflection of his poor statesmanship.

b) Civil War

The overt cause of civil war in 1464 was the royal birth of princess Joanna in 1462. Many disgruntled magnates like the Enríquez and

Manrique families and the Archbishops of Toledo and Seville claimed that she was illegitimate, an opinion that was widely believed even though the only evidence was their conviction that Henry was impotent, an allegation he - naturally enough - consistently denied. When Henry sacked his principal minister, Villena, in 1464 in favour of Pedro González de Mendoza and Beltrán de la Cueva, the alleged father of the princess, the magnates claimed that the King was unfit to rule and pledged their support for his step-brother, Alfonso. In June 1465 several nobles attended the so-called 'Farce of Ávila', when the ceremonial deposition of Henry IV was symbolically enacted and Alfonso proclaimed as the rightful king.[3] Villena joined the opposition and Castile divided into two mutually hostile camps: the northern provinces and León supported Henry, but ranged against him was the rest of his kingdom, including the most prosperous towns, the leading bishops and the military orders. For four years Henry's cause seemed hopeless but he was saved by the habitually suspicious nobility, a general recognition that peace was preferable to war, and by Alfonso's unexpected death from plague in 1468.

A skilful statesman could have defused this potentially explosive situation before it got out of control by asserting his authority, reaching a compromise with the nobility and resolving the succession. At first Henry grasped the nettle. In 1468 he recalled Villena, recognised Isabella, his step-sister, as heir-presumptive, and agreed to her marriage to Ferdinand of Aragon which took place in October 1469. Castilian magnates were delighted. Many believed that union with Aragon was the kingdom's best course of action to prevent a continuance of civil war. Yet instead of keeping his word, within months Henry transferred his support to Joanna and disowned Isabella's claim to the throne. Civil disorder would rack Castile for the next ten years.

c) The Economy

It would not be an exaggeration to say that the physical features of Castile encouraged regional separatism. Nearly half of the kingdom comprised a plateau, 1,000 metres high, known as the *meseta*, surrounded and interspersed by ranges of mountains and unnavigable rivers. Apart from narrow coastal strips and river valleys, there was little fertile land, while hot dry summers made farming difficult. Agricultural techniques were primitive and subsistence farming prevailed in most areas outside the principal cities. Galicia, Vizcaya and Asturias in the north were forested regions and regularly imported cereals. León and central Castile were dominated by herdsmen and sheep farmers, and in the west the military orders owned extensive cattle and sheep ranches. Andalucía in the south was the most fertile area, enjoying a warm climate and advanced irrigation techniques along the river Guadalquivir. Its principal city of Seville was the most populous in Castile.

Although figures are necessarily inexact on account of the absence of censuses, the kingdom's population was probably little more than four million and only a few cities like Seville, Valladolid, Córdoba, Salamanca, Toledo and Burgos appear to have had more than 10,000 people.

Most Castilian towns owed their prosperity to sheep farming. The profitability of pastoral farming, the introduction of merino sheep from north Africa in the fourteenth century, the expansion of farms as lands were seized from the Muslims and the protection afforded the owners by the Mesta, the sheep farmers' guild - all these contributed to an explosion in the Castilian woollen trade. By the 1460s there were some 11 million non-migratory sheep as well as eight million that trekked seasonally along the main sheepwalks of Castile. Burgos lay at the centre of the woollen industry in northern Castile, transporting wool to Bilbao for export to Bruges and importing cloth for the textile industry in Segovia, Toledo and Cuenca. Nearby towns derived their livelihood from this trade. Medina del Campo and Villalón were commercial fairs and the northern ports of Santander and Biscay traded in wool, cloth, wine and metals with northern Europe. In the south, Andalucía imported gold, sugar and slaves from the Mediterranean and north Africa, and exported wool, wine, fruit and oil to northern Europe. There were even a few small-scale artisan industries such as shipbuilding and soap in Seville, and mercury mining near Almáden. Although much of Seville's commerce and finance was in the hands of immigrant Genoese families, a trend that would grow throughout the sixteenth century, some nobles were engaged in commercial activities. The Enríquez family, for example, invested in the soap industry and the Medinaceli in salt. Overall the economy of Castile was on an upward curve and close to overtaking Catalonia, its commercial rival. Significantly very little trade occurred with the Aragonese kingdoms: transport was difficult, tolls operated at the border and Catalonia preferred to develop its Italian and Mediterranean links.

d) Society

Castile was a status-conscious society. The aristocracy, nobility, clergy and royal office-holders had privileges in so far as they did not perform manual work, were exempt from direct taxation and had extensive legal rights. For instance, they could not be imprisoned for debt, sent to the galleys or tortured. Lawyers, doctors, merchants and town officials were also privileged in that they could vote and enjoyed a social standing far superior to that of the vast majority of workers, servants and peasantry. Each member of society aspired to improve his status with the ultimate goal of attaining *hidalguía,* the lowest rank of nobility. Few achieved it of course, although Henry's sale of *hidalguía* certainly encouraged more urban groups to believe it was a possibility.

Perhaps as much as 97 per cent of land in Castile was owned by three per cent of the population. The principal noble and ecclesiastical offices were held by just 15 families whose power was immense. The Fajardo family dominated Murcia, the Mendozas much of New Castile and the Zúnigas Extremadura. Most of this land had been seized from the Muslims and granted to the nobles by the Crown in the Middle Ages but, as the Reconquest slowed down in the course of the fourteenth century, Castilian kings began to grant them legal and fiscal privileges within their estates, known as *señoríos*. The Crown's aim was to increase royal control but the result was an increase in noble independence. Furthermore the practice of bequeathing property solely to the eldest heir was well established and ensured that family estates could not be so easily broken up. In his attempt to curry favour with his nobility, Henry IV sold off more royal land than any other Trastámara and unwittingly presented the nobility with the chance to raise their tenants' rents and claim lands from nearby towns and monasteries. Most towns were dominated by the nobility: Gibraltar, for example, was controlled by Medina Sidonia and Cádiz by the Ponce de León, but some towns like Salamanca and Baeza successfully resisted assaults on their liberties. In fact Castile had never experienced a feudal system and attempts by some nobles to increase their control over rural and urban groups led to social tension and conflict.

Perhaps 80 per cent of Castilian society was peasantry. Although peasants were legally free, most worked such poor quality land that they could not maintain their annual rents and taxes and so fell into debt. Some migrated to towns in search of food and employment but opportunities were limited. Domestic servants, for instance, were bought on the open market from slave-traders. Africa, Russia and the Balkans were the main sources of supply and slaves were commonly used as agricultural labourers, galley oarsmen and prostitutes.

e) Religion

It was widely believed in the fifteenth century that the Church in Castile was in urgent need of reform. Many of the upper clergy lived worldly lives at odds with their Christian ideals. The primate, the Archbishop of Toledo, maintained an army of 1,000 men, controlled 19,000 vassals and was more interested in political affairs than in the spiritual welfare of his diocese. Don Luis de Acuña, Bishop of Burgos, fathered two illegitimate sons; the Archbishop of Santiago could raise more than 3,000 troops, and at Palencia some 20 per cent of the cathedral clergy kept concubines. The conduct of many parish clergy appears to have been little better. Reports of unordained clerics who claimed legal privileges to which they were not entitled, and of poorly educated and married priests, were legion. It should be noted, however, that such complaints were often a reflection of the high ideals of the academic visitors; to most people, a priest who lived with a concubine or who fathered a child only became reprehensible if he behaved indiscreetly or if he was very harsh on similar failings in his flock.

The condition of the regular clergy also varied considerably. Cistercian and Benedictine houses in Galicia, which was a particularly lax province, contained monks who had few books, knew little Latin and kept women. On the other hand, the rich Hieronimite monastery of Guadalupe near Toledo and the Benedictine Congregation of San Benito in Valladolid were widely respected. An important reform movement was associated with the Observant Franciscan friars who distanced themselves from the Conventual Franciscans as the latter had abandoned their pastoral and community work in favour of monastic seclusion. The Observants began to apply their rules more strictly in the course of the fifteenth century, a practice that was later imitated by Dominican and Augustinian orders, and one which provided inspiration for reforms under the Catholic Monarchs.

In a climate of minimal religious instruction, popular beliefs assumed greater importance than official creeds. The cult of saints, especially St Anne and the Virgin Mary, flourished as did festivals, processions and pilgrimages. Belief in purgatory lay at the heart of popular religious dramas, penitential sermons and personal redemption. Local celebrations were often arranged by confraternities that assisted the poor, sick and orphans, and provided prayers for the souls of deceased members. These organised activities had been founded by town guilds and were largely outside the control of the Church.

In the eleventh century Castilians had begun to attack the Muslims in an attempt to recover their occupied lands, and by 1264 all but the Emirate of Granada had been won back. Since then the frontier had not moved and a spirit of *convivencia* (coexistence) prevailed. The Emir paid an annual tribute to the King of Castile, prisoners were regularly exchanged and frontier disputes were resolved by judges appointed from both Christian and Muslim towns. The spirit of Reconquest, however, lived on in Hispanic literature and in the dreams of warring knights. Even the lacklustre Henry IV had encouraged six frontier raids in the 1450s, although they had met with little success.

During their occupation of the peninsula, the Muslims had encouraged Jews to settle in Castile and practise their faith and culture. The advancing Christians in contrast took a less tolerant view towards alien groups, and expelled or converted the surviving Muslims and Jews. By the fifteenth century few *Mudéjars* (Muslims under Christian rule) remained but large Jewish communities had to decide whether to be converted, and so become *Conversos,* or to continue in the knowledge that they would not be allowed the legal, political and social rights enjoyed by Christians. An estimated 150,000 Jews lived mainly in towns in enclosed communities. Most worked as financiers, tax collectors, administrators, doctors and physicians. Indeed in the biased opinion of one chronicler: 'They never wanted to take manual work, ploughing or digging or walking the fields with the herds ... but only jobs in the towns, so as to sit around making money without doing much work.'[4] While there may have been some truth behind this generalisation, allegations of Jewish cannibalism and necromancy were unproven. *Conversos* were especially despised because they could hold public office and several, like the Maluendas in Burgos and Arias in Segovia, exercised great financial influence controlling the Treasury of the Crown and the military orders.

A sense of religious coexistence remained in Castile but racial tension was always near the surface. Although the fifteenth century did not see anything like the anti-Semitic massacres of the pogrom of 1391, when thousands of Jews were forced into conversion, towns like Toledo and Seville with large Jewish communities saw intermittent outbreaks of violence. Furthermore the belief, held by many Christians, that large numbers of *Conversos* were really false converts and that the purity of their blood (*limpieza de sangre*) should be investigated, endangered peaceful relations.

f) Culture

Castile had two universities at Salamanca and Valladolid but neither had much impact on the intellectual and cultural development of the kingdom. A revival of interest in the works of the classical Greek philosopher Aristotle and the medieval theologian Thomas Aquinas by scholars at Salamanca confirmed orthodox Christian views of religion and philosophy and rejected both the 'new learning' from the Netherlands and humanism from Italy. More progressive ideas came from Castilian nobles and *Conversos*. The Marquis of Santillana (d. 1458) composed poetry in the style of Dante, Juan de Mena (d. 1456) imitated Virgil, and Alonso, Bishop of Burgos (d. 1456), translated Seneca and Cicero into Castilian. In painting and sculpture, French, Flemish and German influences were more apparent than any native style, and the architectural features of public buildings, palaces and town fortifications reflected the much admired Islamic civilization. The fifteenth-century Italian Renaissance had so far had little impact on Castile. The Castilian language at least gave the regions a degree of commonality, although the numerous dialectal variations were a continuing source of cultural diversity. In Galicia, for example, a variant of Portuguese and Castilian was spoken.

g) Foreign Relations

At the end of the fourteenth century, Castile and France were political and economic allies. Each regarded Portugal and Aragon with varying degrees of hostility, but by the mid-fifteenth century diplomatic relations had changed. France and Aragon competed for Mediterranean trade and territory in the Pyrenees, neither of which held much attraction to Castile. Portugal showed less inclination to interfere in Castilian politics and, although it had yielded its claims to the Canaries, it was unwilling to concede control over the kingdoms of Africa. What increasingly concerned Castile were challenges to her overseas trade. Basque fishermen clashed with the French, Bilbao merchants with the German Hanseatic League, and Sevillian traders with the Portuguese.

3 Aragon

a) The Crown and its Administration

The kingdom of Aragon had been ruled by another branch of the Trastámara family since 1412, and by John II since 1458. The Crown comprised the three kingdoms of Aragon, Catalonia, Valencia, the Mediterranean islands of Sicily, Sardinia and the Balearics (Majorca, Minorca, Ibiza), and Navarre which had been acquired by marriage in 1425 but was disputed by Castile and France. Unlike the unitary kingdom of Castile, Aragon was a federation of states, each of which held unique political features that the Crown was obliged to respect. The Cortes actually swore an oath of loyalty at the King's coronation which was conditional upon his observing 'all our liberties and laws; and, if not, not'. The idea that the King entered a *pactos* or contract with his subjects and ruled with their consent had been established in the thirteenth century. The Catalan philosopher Francesc Eiximensis (d. 1409) could therefore claim that 'he should not be king who does not hold to and observe the law', and Pere Belluga, a Valencian lawyer, declared in 1441 that the Crown's authority was limited by 'Christian ethics, Natural Law, local customs, and pacts with the people'.[5] The people of Barcelona, the capital of Catalonia, regarded their ruler as a count rather than a king and would only swear fealty to him if he first promised to observe the laws of their kingdom.

In marked contrast to Castile, kings of Aragon had limited power. This was exemplified in their relations with representative assemblies. Each Cort(e)s was different in composition and procedure. The Aragonese Cortes, for instance, regularly met in Zaragoza and represented four estates - the aristocracy, lesser nobility, clergy and towns. Grievances were considered before money was voted and consent was necessary before any laws were approved. Unlike Castile, a standing committee known as the *Diputación* spoke for the people when the Cortes was not in session and a Justiciar, who held office for life and was independent of the King, ensured their laws (or *fueros*) were not invaded by the Crown. The Catalonian Corts comprised three estates - the nobles, clergy and towns - and had to be convened at least every three years. As in Aragon, effective power resided with a committee of six, the *Diputación del General*, who organised the collection of subsidies, authorised legislation and guarded existing rights. Valencia also had three estates and a *Diputación*, and Sardinia, Sicily and Navarre all had assemblies based on the Catalan-Aragon model. Sometimes the Crown convened a General Cortes when representatives from the kingdoms of Valencia, Catalonia and Aragon met together but even then each of them acted independently.

The inevitable absence of the monarch from several kingdoms at any one time saw the establishment of royal governors and lieutenants and, from the late fourteenth century, viceroys who ruled in the King's name. A chancellor presided over the royal council and each kingdom had its own council, financial and judicial administrations. Although there were courts of appeal in each realm, disputes between the Crown and its subjects were resolved by the Justiciar. A deeply entrenched federal tradition ran through all aspects of political life and made any future centralisation difficult to achieve. Effective political power rested with the towns and cities, not with the Crown and nobles as in Castile. Barcelona, Zaragoza and Valencia, and large towns such as Gerona and Lérida held public assemblies which appointed magistrates and councillors. Any attempt by the Crown to influence local appointments appears to have been resisted and some towns like Gerona and Vich had even introduced balloting to break the control of oligarchic families over municipal offices. Moreover, there was no comparable institution to the Castilian *corregidor,* who was such a valuable crown servant in Castile.

b) The Economy

The population of the Crown of Aragon had been slowly rising since the Black Death and was probably about one million in the late fifteenth century. However, there were significant demographic and economic variations within the kingdoms. Aragon's population, which was probably about 250,000, was growing but it had no large towns other than Zaragoza. Moreover, as it was a land-locked kingdom with poor soil and rocky terrain, and heavily dependent upon trade with Navarre and Catalonia, its pastoral economy was unlikely to be the driving force behind any future economic growth. Valencia, in contrast, was a thriving kingdom. Its capital was by 1460 the largest city in the Crown of Aragon. Rice, sugar cane and fruit were grown in the irrigated areas and its oranges, raisins and pomegranates were exported to northern Europe. It did, however, need to import wheat and oil but its economic prospects seemed favourable as Italian merchants moved more of their trade there in the second half of the fifteenth century.

Catalonia's economy was in a state of decline. Its population was falling from an estimated 350,000 in 1378 to 300,000 by 1497, principally due to the decline of Barcelona. From 1350 to 1460

Barcelona was the main centre for trade in the western Mediterranean. Its ships transported Sicilian and Majorcan wheat, Sardinian silver and salt, and wines, spices and cereals along the Provençal coast to Italy. It imported Adriatic goods, Russian and Far Eastern silk, spices and gold, English tin and wool, Flemish textiles and fish, and African gold and coral. (At the height of its prosperity in the early fifteenth century, its maritime insurance, municipal bank, guilds, joint-stock companies and Consulado surpassed all other Mediterranean ports.) Historians dispute whether or not there were signs of serious economic decay before 1460: Pierre Vilar and Jaime Vicens Vives believe that the economy was struggling whereas J.N. Hillgarth sees little sign of decline, but all agree that the impact of civil war in Catalonia throughout this decade was devastating.[6] It had been beset by intermittent plague, currency devaluations, increasing bankruptcies and a decline in Majorcan trade, but civil war saw French and Italian merchants transfer more and more of their trade to Valencia. Indeed even Catalonians moved some of their business investments to the southern kingdom. Barcelona remained a major port but its days of supremacy had passed. Significantly, the absence of any economic union between the kingdoms - they had their own currencies and levied tolls at their borders and ports of entry - served to underline the relish with which Valencians watched the decline of their trading rival Barcelona.

c) Society

The potential for social conflict in the Crown of Aragon was greater than in Castile where the aristocracy exercised more power. There were only 20 titled nobles compared with 62 in Castile and the knights were more influential in the localities. They dominated most town councils and their representation since the thirteenth century in the Cortes ensured they retained control. Lawyers, notaries, merchants and master-craftsmen called for electoral reform, and with it economic and social advancement, while lesser merchants, labourers and artisans pressed for representation in urban affairs. In Barcelona, for instance, the five city councillors were elected from a select number of 'honoured citizens', a category which excluded most of the population.

Peasant conditions on noble and clerical estates varied considerably. In Aragon greater nobles had kept firm control over their tenant farmers but less prosperous rural landlords struggled to survive and many peasants had seen their feudal obligations abolished. Indeed in Valencia, where there were many *Mudéjar* settlements, cooperatives had emerged and there was little sign of peasant unrest. Catalonia, in contrast, had a long feudal tradition and agrarian conditions were ripe for exploitation. Nobles with small estates in the north-east were eager to make the more prosperous peasants pay more rents, whereas the poorer *remensa* peasantry sought to revoke their unpopular feudal services. Generally the Crown sided with the peasantry in an attempt to weaken noble and patrician control, but such intrusive behaviour was not welcomed by the landowners: in 1455 feudal practices were abolished by royal decree only to be re-introduced by the Corts seven years later.

Civil war broke out in 1462, occasioned by a mixture of political, social and economic motives. Wealthy merchants and knights were intent upon giving the *Diputación* more power by winning control of Barcelona's council; less privileged groups countered this faction by supporting the Crown in its attempt to re-impose its authority over the city. In Barcelona the *Busca*, a group of merchants and shopkeepers, was challenging the ruling property owners and wealthy merchants, known as the *Biga*, for economic and political dominance. In the country the *remensa* peasantry revolted in the hope that the Crown would free them from their feudal obligations. For the next ten years John II and the *Diputación* fought for control. The King enlisted the help of Louis XI of France who, in return for troops, held the border counties of Roussillon and Cerdagne. When John failed to meet the full cost of the troops in 1463, France retained the counties: this led the *Diputación* to claim the King was willing to betray his own subjects. Its behaviour, however, was equally dubious when it too looked for foreign assistance. Eventually its hopes rested on René of Anjou, Duke of Provence, while John II sought to isolate French involvement by forming an alliance with England and Burgundy. Diplomatic pressure took time to work. In the interim both sides won indecisive battles but what proved to be of far greater significance was the marriage of Ferdinand, John's only surviving son, to Isabella of Castile in October 1469 (see page 20). The Enríquez family, powerful and loyal supporters of the princess, immediately offered troops to the King of Aragon and within three years he had restored peace to Catalonia.

d) Religion

Although there have not been many detailed studies of the Church in Aragon, conditions similar to those in Castile appear to have existed. Cases of clerical abuse were viewed more seriously by learned visitors than by unlearned parishioners, and some clergy performed their spiritual duties competently while a few were notoriously corrupt. The Archbishop of Tarragona (1445-89), for example, committed incest, the Bishop of Valencia, Rodrigo Borgia, was absent from his see for more than 30 years and ecclesiastical landlords in Catalonia were known to excommunicate tenants who fell behind with their rents. Popular religion was as divergent as in Castile. The large number of confraternities in principal towns attests to the strong belief in purgatory and many watched religious dramas and processions or went on pilgrimages. The Benedictine monastery of Montserrat in Catalonia, which held the shrine of the Virgin Mary, was the principal centre for pilgrims. Popular preaching largely fell to travelling friars. Of course, some orders were more active than others. The Hieronimites and Observant Friars appear to have been more interested in meeting the needs of ordinary people than were the Carthusians and Dominicans.

Christian attitudes to *Mudéjars* and Jews were markedly different from those in Castile. The Reconquest had been accomplished in the thirteenth century and *Mudéjars* and *Moriscos* (Muslims who became Christians) assimilated into Aragonese society. The widespread admiration for Muslim cultural and technical achievements encouraged Christians in Valencia and Aragon, where most of the *Mudéjars* lived, to let them retain their civil and religious customs. By the fifteenth century the *Mudéjars* numbered some 300,000 and were too large to be easily driven out; furthermore, their advanced farming techniques and craftsmanship, as well as their willingness to till the soil, explains why they had not been persecuted and why *convivencia* was so widespread. The same story of coexistence was true for Jews and *Conversos;* but, unlike the *Mudéjars*, they were viewed as a social and financial threat. Few lived in the countryside and only small numbers, perhaps 30,000, worked in the towns, principally in Zaragoza, Teruel, Gerona and Calatayud. Racial violence did occasionally erupt, although never as fiercely as in Castile, but the existence of a Catalan inquisition, set up in the thirteenth century to investigate *Conversos* and long since abandoned, indicated how intense anti-Semitic feelings could become.

e) Culture

The Crown of Aragon was linguistically and culturally diverse. The prolonged presence of the Muslims in Aragon and early expulsion from Old Catalonia probably explains the dialectal and phonetic differences between Aragonese, Catalan and Romance (Romance had French-Catalan origins and was spoken by a minority within the Crown of Aragon). In the fifteenth century Catalan was the dominant language within the three kingdoms but Catalonian culture was more heterogeneous. The Muslim imprint on architecture and art remained a strong influence in Barcelona, Valencia, Zaragoza and Majorca but Italian trade brought Renaissance ideas, including humanism, the printing press and new artistic styles. Thus the Catalan novel *Tirant lo Blanc* by Martorell (d. 1468) bore Italian influences, the first printed books appeared in Barcelona and Valencia in the 1470s, and the court archivist copied and annotated classical manuscripts in the manner of Italian humanists. Painting, however, still reflected Flemish schools of art and the leading Catalan painter, Jaime Huguet was in many respects a disciple of Roger van der Weyden. Two universities had been established in the fifteenth century at Lérida and Huesca and a third opened in Zaragoza in 1474 but their impact upon education at levels below the intellectually elite was minimal. Indeed, it was a similar story to Castile's.

f) Foreign Relations

Italy's influence upon the Crown of Aragon in foreign affairs was similarly profound. John's control of Sicily, Sardinia, the Balearics, and for a short period until 1458 Naples, saw him aspire to extend his Italian possessions possibly with the aim of seizing Milan or Genoa. Such ambitions brought the Aragonese Trastámaras within the orbit of the French House of Valois. They responded by probing his control of the Pyrenees. The kingdom of Navarre had been ruled by John since 1425 but in 1462 he disinherited his son in favour of his daughter and her French husband. As a result the kingdom had competing claimants for the next 50 years. The Catalonian counties of Roussillon and Cerdagne had also been relinquished to France, and John never recovered them. In 1469 Aragon was busy constructing alliances against France, and Ferdinand's marriage to Isabella should be seen as John's ace in the pack, designed to bring Castile into his fold. Given that it was accomplished against Henry IV's wishes, it was a major coup.

4 Conclusion

The differences between the Hispanic kingdoms within and beyond the Iberian peninsula were considerable. Not since the Roman occupation had the country, then known as Hispania, been under one rule. Divided by language and religion, governed by different political institutions and ruled by monarchs with conflicting foreign interests, the Crowns of Castile and Aragon apart from their Trastámaran dynasties appear to have had little in common. Furthermore, their economies were quite different in their structure and levels of progress. Catalonia was in decline while Valencia was staging a recovery; and in Castile, the traditional pastoral economy in the north and centre was falling behind the more diverse commercial activities in the south. In fact both Aragon and Castile were developing dual economies, and for different reasons. There were also profound social differences within and between the kingdoms. The Castilian nobility was wealthier and the peasantry more liberated than in Aragon, where there were fewer nobles but more serfs and larger cities.

The fourteenth-century Castilian historian Pero López de Ayala believed that each kingdom had its own identity, an opinion shared by the Valencian lawyer, Pere Belluga, writing in 1441. Some court propagandists like Alonso de Cartagena (d. 1456) claimed Castilian superiority over the other kingdoms averring that 'kings of Spain descend from the House of Castile', but this was a minority view. Similarly, few agreed with the Catalan historian, Joan Margarit i Pau (d. 1484), when he proclaimed that the King of Aragon was the heir of the Goths, who once ruled the peninsula. Separatism was a more powerful force than unity in fifteenth-century Spain, where there appears to have been no sense of national identity.[7] It is therefore hard to agree with Ramón Menéndez Pidal that 'the national desire to reconstruct the unity of the kingdom of the Goths showed itself in every way, even before the political fusion of the two kingdoms was accomplished'.[8] Castile rivalled Aragon, Valencia resented Catalonia, and their failure to drive out the infidel from Granada was proof of their disharmony and the disunity within the peninsula. Few observers could have predicted how the marriage of Isabella and Ferdinand in 1469 would change the direction of Spanish history. In fact, the full significance of the union would not be appreciated by contemporaries until the 1480s, although it is now clear that its impact was more immediate in so far as it enabled both Isabella and Ferdinand to secure their thrones more easily. And this is the theme of the next chapter.

References

1   J.H. Mariéjol, *The Spain of Ferdinand and Isabella,* trans. and ed. B.Keen (New Jersey, 1961), p. 117.
2   In 1474 only 15 per cent of revenue reached the Crown. M.A.Ladero Quesada, *La Hacienda Real castellana en el siglo xv* (Laguna, 1973), p. 42.
3   A. Mackay, 'Ritual and Propaganda in Fifteenth-Century Castile', *Past and Present Society,* 55 (1972), pp. 3-43.
4   Andrés Bernáldez, *Historia de los reyes católicos D. Fernando y D. Isabel* vol. 2 (Seville, 1870), Ch. xliii.
5   T.N. Bisson, *The Medieval Crown of Aragon* (Oxford University Press, 1986), p. 165.
6   J.N. Hillgarth, *The Spanish Kingdoms, 1410-1516,* vol. 2 (Clarendon Press, Oxford, 1978), p. 44.
7   Helmut Koenigsberger, 'National Consciousness in Early Modern Spain', in *Politicians and Virtuosi: Essays in Early Modern History* (The Hambledon Press, London, 1986), pp. 121-47.
8   Ramón Menéndez Pidal, *Historia de España,* xv (Madrid, 1964), p. ix.

Making notes on 'Spain in the Reigns of Isabella and Ferdinand, 1474-1516'

Before you start to make notes on this and later chapters, you should decide exactly what it is that you wish to record. This chapter, for example, offers a background survey of Castile and Aragon in 1469, and, if you are interested mainly in the reigns of Isabella and Ferdinand, then detailed notes will not be required. Instead you should write brief notes on each sub-section to reassure yourself that you have identified and understood the main issues. More specialised chapters, on the other hand, such as Chapter 3, 'Government and Administration under the Catholic Monarchs, 1474-1516', will need more detailed treatment. You should only record the main facts relevant to your purpose, and set them out neatly and clearly to enable you to memorise them more easily.

Distinguish between facts, explanations and judgements; and if a historian suggests a possible interpretation, carefully consider it before writing it down.

The headings and sub-headings will help you organise your material and the conclusion, which draws together the key points in the chapter, provides you with an opportunity to think for yourself and to reach your own verdicts. Look at the study diagrams at the end of each chapter. They summarise the principal themes in a visual form and may provide you with further ideas about the significance of the events. Can you think, for instance, how the ring of outer boxes in the Summary - the Hispanic Kingdoms in 1469 (page 18) - might be sub-divided? Make good use of the maps and illustrations: these will repay careful study and will aid your understanding. It may also help you to construct a time-line for each chapter: this gives you a chronological framework, which is so important in establishing the sequence of events and in your understanding of the links between cause and effect in history.

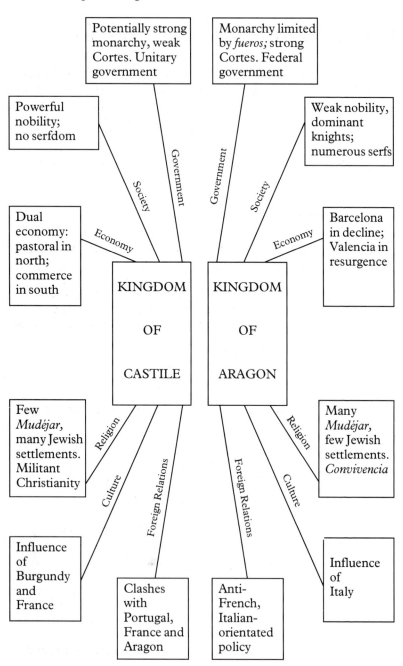

Summary - The Hispanic Kingdoms in 1469

CHAPTER 2

Securing the Throne, 1469-79

The decade of the 1470s was a vital period in the lives of Isabella and Ferdinand. It witnessed the end of the civil wars in Castile and Aragon, the failure of attempts to depose Isabella, and the start of the reforms which set Castile on the road to recovery. This chapter begins by examining the significance of their marriage. It then considers the impact of the wars in Aragon and Castile, before assessing the work of several court chroniclers and, finally, considering the key issue of the relative importance of the various factors which enabled Isabella to secure her throne.

1 The Marriage

In the late 1460s Henry IV of Castile had hoped that his half-sister Isabella would marry the King of Portugal and cement an alliance with this stable country, but she showed little interest in this man who was 19 years her senior and already had several children by his first marriage. In fact, her preferred choice was Ferdinand of Aragon. Her half-brother and father had married Aragonese princesses and King John II of Aragon was married to the Admiral of Castile's daughter, Joanna

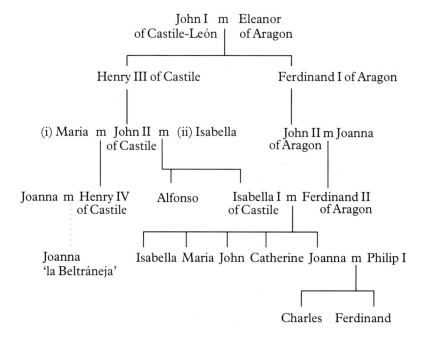

The Trastámara dynasty

Enríquez. Moreover the Enríquez family, who were staunch supporters of Isabella, had resented Portugal's interference in Castilian affairs. Many nobles therefore felt that their own interests would be better served by a union between Isabella and Ferdinand, John's eldest son (see the diagram on page 19).

In October 1469, the 18-year-old Isabella met the 17-year-old Ferdinand for the first time: within hours they were married. While the young couple spent the next few weeks in each other's company, their political advisers formulated the terms of the marriage contract. It acknowledged Isabella as the rightful heir of Castile and León; she would have no power in Aragon, nor Ferdinand in Castile; and their children would be educated in Castile. Nothing was said about who would rule her kingdom if she pre-deceased her husband. Ferdinand was told that he must live in Castile, respect its customs, and acknowledge the supremacy of his wife in every decision. He was to supply her with 100,000 gold florins and 4,000 troops if required. Thus the treaty was clearly intended to benefit Castile and in no sense presaged the unification of the two kingdoms. Yet apart from a desire not to compromise Isabella's claim to the Castilian throne by appearing to give parity to the Aragonese prince, the terms also reflect an apprehension felt by many Castilians that John II intended using their resources to further his own ends in Aragon. They knew that he was at war with France, that he had very few resources and was looking for Castilian money and troops to help him achieve a victory in Catalonia and recover his frontier counties.

Over the next few years Ferdinand provided great assistance in helping Isabella gain the throne but claims by Ferdinand's supporters that upon her accession to the Castilian throne he should take precedence and become King of Castile were dismissed by the Queen. Nevertheless in January 1475 it was declared that their seals and banners would bear their arms, that both heads would appear on all coins, and that they would dispense justice together. Three months later, Ferdinand was granted full authority in Castile in Isabella's absence 'to provide, command, create and ordain'. She was mainly concerned with holding onto her throne and needed her husband's assistance to head her army but not at the cost of alienating her supporters by making him too strong. When Ferdinand became King of Aragon in 1479, the monarchs announced that they would rule their kingdoms jointly and, henceforth, they would be known as 'Prince Ferdinand and Princess Isabella, by the grace of God, King and Queen of Castile, León, Aragon, Sicily, Toledo, Valencia, Galicia, Mallorca, Seville, Cardona, Córdoba, Córsica, Murcia, Jaén, Algarve, Algeciras, Gibraltar, Count and Countess of Barcelona, Lords of Vizcaya and Molina, Dukes of Athens and Naples, Counts of Roussillon and Cerdagne, Marquesses of Oristán and Gociano'![1]

The importance of the marriage in the future unification of Spain is indisputable. In the short term, however, and especially in the 1470s, the advantages of the union favoured Castile rather than Aragon. Ferdinand directed military operations against rebellious towns and played a major part in defeating the Portuguese armies and the supporters of Joanna 'la Beltráneja', the rival claimant to the Castilian throne. Equally important was the absence of any intrigue or intervention by Aragonese nobles in the Castilian succession crisis. This had not always been the case in recent years and the newly acquired friendship, in no small part a consequence of the marriage, was one of the most significant factors in explaining Isabella's eventual triumph.

2 Civil War in Castile, 1469-74

In 1469 most Castilian towns had been loyal to Henry IV and his daughter Joanna; only a few towns like Valladolid and Tordesillas, and a small number of grandees like the Mendozas and the Archbishop of Toledo were willing to back Isabella's right to succeed the King. Then, in the course of 1470, circumstances changed dramatically in her favour. In October she had a daughter, and in the same month, Charles Duke of Berry, who had been considered as a possible husband for Joanna, died. The 19-year-old Isabella and her 18-year-old husband were more favourably placed than Joanna, who was only nine. Even now, the fate of Isabella rested largely in the hands of the Castilian grandees. Most had no wish to harm her and saw that she could best be used as a political pawn to extract privileges from the King. Her position was strengthened in December 1471 when the Pope ratified her marriage to Ferdinand. As they were second cousins, they had been illegally co-habiting for nearly two years and had needed a papal dispensation to overcome their blood-ties.

Slowly support for Isabella began to grow. Marvin Lunenfeld has suggested that many towns rallied to her cause in 1471 when she pledged never to alienate Crown land.[2] Nobles, eager to expand their estates, presented a real danger to the independence of many towns, and so this offer of protection from overmighty nobles proved an attractive incentive, and led to some twelve towns backing her. Another important gain was the defection of Pedro González de Mendoza. He had made it known that he desired above all things to be a cardinal and, aware that the new pope and his papal legate in Valencia were pro-Aragonese, transferred his support to Ferdinand. When he gained his cardinal's hat in 1472, he was convinced it was a result of Ferdinand's influence, and by the end of the year the entire Mendoza family was ready to support Isabella.

The Duke of Medina Sidonia and André de Cabrera declared their allegiance in 1473. If their motives were personal and their loyalty far from reliable, such defections certainly strengthened Isabella's cause. Medina Sidonia was really interested in securing royal privileges granted by Henry and increasing his power in Seville. Cabrera, on the other hand, held the *alcázar* of Segovia which contained the Crown's treasure. The city was threatened by the Marquis of Villena and rather than submit to this overmighty noble or ineffectual king, Cabrera sought the protection of Isabella and Ferdinand. Segovia was a major stronghold (see the illustration below). Note that its high walls, circular towers and hill-top site made it extremely difficult to assault, so its defection was one of the turning-points in the war. Moreover, in the following year, Tordesillas followed suit. Segovia and Tordesillas were politically and psychologically important gains for Isabella.

The old King, Henry IV, perhaps aware of the rising tide of support for his sister in 1474, agreed to meet her at Segovia and finally acknowledged her right to succeed to the Castilian throne. This declaration, together with the sudden death of Villena in October, must have made it seem to Isabella as if victory was at hand. Villena had been a thorn in everyone's flesh and, as the King's chief supporter and guardian of Joanna, had consistently exploited the Crown. Yet Henry displayed his customary mixture of generosity and recklessness when he promised Diego, Villena's son, the Mastership of Santiago. It was one of Henry's last acts before he died in December, and one destined to cause trouble after his death. The Mastership was an immensely powerful

The alcázar *at Segovia*

office and Diego's claim was bound to be contested. That he also assumed his father's guardianship of Joanna in Madrid increased his political importance as well as his unpopularity.

3 The War of Succession, 1475-79

Isabella was crowned Queen in Segovia on 13 December 1474 but her throne was far from secure. Opposition from three sources had to be overcome before she could relax: from a number of disaffected magnates, from numerous disloyal towns and from foreign supporters of the rival claimant Joanna.

a) The Castilian Grandees

Well before she became Queen, Isabella had gone some way towards building up a powerful bloc of grandees, bishops and towns. Now it was expedient to make further deals. Cardinal Mendoza was promised the chancellorship and his brother was created Duke of Infantado; Enríquez was awarded the honorific title of Admiral of Castile and Velasco was confirmed as Constable of Castile. The Queen's right to dispense royal patronage was proving a valuable weapon in her armoury. Not only were nobles and bishops drawn into Isabella's circle of favourites but her supporters could reasonably expect to have their loyalty rewarded in the future. The Count of Benavente, for instance, had previously served Henry but now offered her his support. Other nobles, perhaps uncertain whether to rally to Isabella or to Joanna, may have been won over by Isabella's promise to confirm all *hidalgos* (grants of nobility) conferred by Henry IV and by her guarantee that the right to collect *mercedes* (financial grants) awarded by the Crown since 1464 would be enforced. More importantly, she promised to investigate widespread complaints that only a small percentage of the money collected by royal tax farmers ever reached the nobles. In December 1474, the Aragonese ambassador had ominously informed his King that 'the nobles of Castile may accept this succession but this is so in some cases because they can do nothing else ... they have their ears open and are ready to do as much harm as they can'.[3] While it remains true that some grandees like Medina Sidonia were fair weather friends, the situation in fact was not so bleak.

Those grandees who openly supported Joanna consisted of a small group of disillusioned nobles and bishops. The young Marquis of Villena was the key figure. He held numerous castles and vast estates between Toledo and Murcia, and was the guardian of princess Joanna. Indeed, the 13-year-old girl was effectively his prisoner in Madrid castle and would, he declared, only be released to get married. On a personal note, Villena hoped to secure the Mastership of Santiago to consolidate his power in Extremadura and New Castile. The death of the Master in

1476 gave him his opportunity but he failed to be elected and for the moment submitted to the Queen. Most of his fortresses were handed to the Crown and any of his governors who demurred were forced into submission by royal troops. Villena accepted a pardon but a year later he was again in rebellion and only surrendered when his fortified town of Escalona was captured.

Carrillo, Archbishop of Toledo, declared himself in favour of Joanna not so much because he disliked Isabella but because he was annoyed about not becoming Cardinal of Castile. Since his arch-rival Mendoza had declared himself for the Crown, Carrillo in 1476 adopted a contrary stance. News of his defection was a serious blow. He controlled over 19,000 vassals, and more than 2,000 troops in 20 castles and fortified towns throughout his archdiocese. However, having sustained a near-fatal injury at the battle of Olmedo in 1476, he resolved to stop fighting and two years later, when he lost his right to control the town of Talavera, formally submitted to the Queen. The Duke of Arévalo had aspired to the Mastership of Alcántara and decided in 1476 that his best course of action was to join the Queen. In contrast, the Marquis of Girón, and his cousin the Count of Ureña, were willing to risk everything on the outcome of this war and only acknowledged the Queen when hostilities ceased in 1479.

b) Castilian Towns and Cities

Although only a handful of grandees opposed Isabella in 1474, the position in the towns and cities was less favourable. Rival groups known as *bandos* fought for control of their towns, and most of the north and south, and large areas of the east and centre, were in revolt. Between 1474 and 1476 Isabella used a variety of methods to win over these dissident regions. A favoured strategy was to approach prominent citizens to find out what would most appeal to their town. Some like those in Burgos requested royal protection from nobles who were threatening their liberty. Some towns like Toledo were offered extensive privileges if they submitted, while others like Seville were threatened with commercial and financial penalties if they refused to acknowledge the Queen. Ciudad Rodrigo transferred its loyalty when the keeper of its castle was offered the governorship of the city. The Queen herself visited the troublesome regions of Extremadura and Andalucía in 1477, and they welcomed her promise not to request any more special taxation.

More duplicitous tactics were employed elsewhere. Secret approaches were made to many of the 150,000 vassals on the Marquis of Villena's estates offering them royal protection if they rebelled against him, and similar deals appear to have been made with vassals of other nobles who supported Joanna. Where towns showed no sign of surrender or openly rejected overtures of peace - as at Trujillo and Córdoba - force was employed. Furthermore, Isabella was fully prepared to make an example of anyone who challenged her authority. Juan de Córdoba, for example, was executed in 1476 for holding Toledo's fortress and city gates in the name of the Count of Fuensalida, one of Joanna's supporters.

Once she had gained the loyalty of a town, the Queen usually sent a *corregidor* (civil governor) to safeguard her interest. In 1478, for instance, Francisco de Valdés replaced Alonso de Aguilar, one of Joanna's staunchest supporters in Córdoba. Not every town, however, welcomed the presence of a royal officer and some like Toledo refused to admit one. For the moment, there was little the Queen could do. She lacked the military might and had no wish to disturb a fragile peace by forcing unwanted Crown appointees upon them. In fact, only 44 *corregidores* had been appointed to towns by 1479 but the Queen had won their respect if not their obedience, and the foundations of her future domestic policy had been established.

Marvin Lunenfeld in his study of the Hermandad (see page 39) has demonstrated its importance in strengthening Isabella's control over Castilian towns and helping her to win the War of Succession.[4] As soon as she came to the throne she sent two councillors to the cities of Zamora, Segovia, Salamanca, Burgos and Palencia, to see if they would support the establishment of a general brotherhood. As each had already formed their own *hermandad* and recognised the need to restore order as soon as possible, they were likely to agree. Her decision, therefore, to bring all of the *hermandades* under royal control and establish a Santa Hermandad in 1476 to direct them was a significant step in restoring royal peace. In point of fact, only eight northern towns sent representatives to the first meeting in July but decisions taken at this meeting proved invaluable to the Queen. They promised her money to finance an army of some 2,000 to 3,000 troops and command was given to her husband's Aragonese brother Alonso, Duke of Villahermosa.

The Hermandad was viewed as a temporary measure taken to deal with an emergency and everyone agreed that it would be disbanded when the crisis had passed. As most cities had submitted by the end of 1477 and the challenge from Joanna appeared to have subsided, Isabella no doubt employed all her powers of persuasion to secure its continuance for a further three years. She not only succeeded but also extracted a sizeable grant from the Hermandad. Several grandees, including her close supporter the Duke of Infantado, were sufficiently concerned to call for its abolition, declaring: 'It is a burden on the people and an abomination to the great'.[5] But the Queen ignored their protests and responded aggressively by insisting that any person or corporation who refused to contribute to it would be prosecuted. This 'temporary' institution was to continue until 1498.

The chroniclers Palencia and Pulgar both claimed that without the Hermandad the Queen could not have controlled her aristocracy, but this would appear to be an exaggeration. Although its troops assisted

Ferdinand in 1477 in capturing several of Villena's fortresses, most grandees were far too powerful to be confronted militarily. Nevertheless, by taking control of the rural brotherhoods and turning them into a national militia, the Crown had marshalled an effective force capable of disciplining rebellious towns and maintaining law and order in the countryside. Pulgar, writing in the 1480s, explained:

1 In those days, of tyrannical and thieving men, and other people of evil intent, in the towns, on the roads, and generally in all parts of the kingdom, nobody thought twice about committing any violent crime, nobody thought of obeying, of respecting, or of paying their
5 debts to another. And for this reason the kingdom was full of petty thieves, crimes and violent attacks in all regions, without fear of God or of justice. And so by virtue of the present war, as well as because of the disorders and past wars of the time of Don Enrique [Henry IV], people were so accustomed to such disorder, that the
10 young man assumed the customs and habits, aggressive behaviour and extravagances that youth demands, and pride and decadent customs were perpetuated in everyone's lives; in such a way that the man who showed himself the physically weakest held himself to be inferior. And the citizens, farm labourers and peace-loving men
15 were not their own masters, nor had they recourse to anyone on account of the robberies, attacks, ransoms and other evils which they endured at the hands of the fortress lords, or other robbers or thieves. And each one volunteered to contribute the half of his goods in order to keep his person and his family safe from the
20 threats of death, injuries or kidnappings.
    And it was debated several times in the towns in order to establish some Brotherhoods as well as to give some order amongst these bodies in order to remedy so many ills and violent acts that they had to suffer continually. But they needed a person who had
25 sufficient zeal to carry this out, and there was established a 'congregation' of towns in which orders were set out to put an end to those evils. Since the King and Queen, in spite of the fact that they were punishing [criminals] as far as they were able, owing to the impediment of the war which they were waging against the
30 King of Portugal, they had no time or opportunity to carry out all the remedies that they would have desired.[6]

c) War with Portugal and the Treaty of Alcaçovas

In January 1475 King Alfonso of Portugal announced that he would invade Castile, marry Joanna and crown her Queen. Equally disturbing for Isabella was the news that Louis XI of France intended invading northern Castile. It was clear that the Queen was going to have to fight to keep her throne. Hastily she borrowed what money she could from her grandees, raised 40,000 troops and put her husband in command. The only pitched battle occurred near Toro in March 1476 and, although it was inconclusive, it halted Alfonso and was regarded by Isabella as a victory. Shortly afterwards she convened her first Cortes in celebration. This regal act demonstrated that in spite of the challenge to her throne, she was the rightful queen. Alfonso, in the meantime, took possession of Joanna and returned to Portugal where he learned that the Pope had granted him a dispensation to marry his niece. Less appetising for him was the news that the French had reached an agreement with Isabella not to continue their campaign.

1478 proved to be a vital year. The birth of a son gave Isabella greater security at precisely the moment when Alfonso's fortunes changed for the worse. His second invasion of Castile in 1478 failed and the Papacy revoked its dispensation allowing him to marry Joanna. When Ferdinand became King of Aragon in January 1479, the game was up. At the peace talks concluded in September, Isabella was recognised as Queen of Castile and Alfonso assumed responsibility for Joanna, who, it was later announced, was to become a nun. Portugal renounced all claims to Castile and the Canaries but retained its monopoly of trade and lands in Africa. It proved a satisfying and durable peace. Portugal remained a friendly neighbour and Joanna never again threatened Isabella's hold on the Crown.

4 Civil War and Succession in Aragon, 1469-79

The principal objective behind the marriage of Ferdinand and Isabella as far as King John of Aragon was concerned was to close the diplomatic net around France and bring to an end attempts by Catalonia to break away from his control and displace him with René of Lorraine, a rival claimant. Any potential support from Castile threatened France's northern and eastern frontiers and jeopardised its interests in Italy and the Pyrenees. Louis of France was aware of this and, in any case, depended upon the activities of René, whose death in 1470 brought Catalonia a step closer to peace. The war ended in October 1472 with the fall of Barcelona.

For ten years Catalonia had been racked by civil war. King John did not exaggerate when he declared, 'the Principality is greatly destroyed'. Barcelona's commercial and trading supremacy had passed to the city of Valencia, Crown finances were ruined, and civil unrest smouldered throughout the Aragonese kingdoms. In the aftermath of war the *remensa* peasantry were still disgruntled at not gaining their freedom from oppressive landlords; nobles and knights disputed landownership rights; and arguments continued between the *Diputación* and city of Barcelona over outstanding debts. In addition to these difficulties, the Catalan counties of Roussillon and Cerdagne remained in French hands, and there was no sign that they would be returned. Hope rested with Prince Ferdinand. As in Castile, where chroniclers had foretold Isabella would save their kingdom, so in Catalonia Ferdinand was proclaimed as 'the Holy Father, the Messiah'. At his accession in January 1479, it was believed that a golden age had dawned. In many respects, it was to prove a false dawn.

5 The Role of Contemporary Chroniclers

Throughout the War of Succession, Isabella's chroniclers conducted an extensive propaganda campaign against her rival claimant, Joanna, and the former king, Henry IV. It suited many nobles to believe the rumour that Joanna was the daughter not of the King - who was said to be impotent - but of Beltrán de la Cueva, a royal councillor. Her illegitimacy, which could not be proved and which the King resolutely denied, duly held centre stage in the official accounts of the reign written after his death by his enemies. In Pulgar's opinion, 'Doña Juana was not, nor could be the daughter of the King'.[7] Chroniclers also dwelt upon Henry's political incompetence and the decadent condition of his kingdom. Enríquez de Castillo, in his work *Crónica de Enrique IV,* believed that the King was at fault in letting his grandees and nobles overrun his court and country. Diego de Valera, who supported those same nobles, argued in his *Crónica* (1482) that they were fully justified in taking up arms. Andrés Bernáldez was a little less biased but equally critical of Henry. In the opening chapter of his *Memorias del Reinado de los Reyes Católicos* written in the 1480s, he describes the reign of King Henry:

1 At this juncture envy and covetousness were awakened and avarice was nourished; justice became moribund and force ruled; greed reigned and decadent sensuality spread, and the cruel temptation of sovereignty overcame the humble persuasion of obedience; the
5 customs were mostly dissolute and corrupt. Many people, having forgotten the loyalty and love which they owed their king, and following their own private interests, allowed the common good to decay, so that both private and public welfare perished.
And Our Lord, who sometimes permits evils to exist on the
10 earth in order that each malefactor should be punished according to the extent of his errors, allowed so many wars to break out in the kingdom, that nobody could say that they were exempt from the ills that ensue from them; especially those who were their instigators, who saw themselves in such dangers, that they sought
15 to abandon a great part of that which they had previously held (in the confidence that they would be able to retain it) and left the vain attempts which they had made to increase their estates ... These

wars lasted for the final ten years for which this King reigned. Peaceful men suffered much violence at the hands of new men who
20 rose up and wrought great havoc. The King at this time spent all his treasury and in addition to these expenses gave away without measure almost all the income from his royal inheritance, much of which was taken by those tyrants who abounded at that time; so that the one who had held many treasures and bought many towns
25 and castles fell into such need that he mortgaged many times over the income from his inheritance, merely in order to maintain himself.[8]

The court chroniclers fulfilled their appointed role: they contrasted the honourable Isabella with the duplicious Henry, her strengths with his weaknesses, the legitimacy of her accession with the spurious claims of her opponents. Her qualities were praised and her opponents damned in the name of history. In their biased and retrospective view, 1474 heralded the start of a new era, pre-ordained by God, in which virtue had triumphed over evil.

1 And as soon as they had begun to reign [wrote Pulgar], they administered justice to certain criminals and thieves who in the time of don Enrique had committed many crimes and evils; and these acts which they carried out made the citizens and farmers and
5 all common people, who were desirous of peace, very happy, and these people gave thanks to God, because a time was coming when it pleased him to take pity on these kingdoms, because of the justice that the King and Queen were beginning to execute; because each one could now be lord and master in his own right
10 without fear or suspicion that another might steal from him.[9]

Of course, in the absence of any alternative official reportage, Castilians at the time considered the chronicles as a true record of events. Less easy to understand is why subsequent generations of historians have so readily and uncritically repeated the panegyrics. As late as 1898, J.H. Mariéjol could declare, 'Anarchy reached its height under Enrique IV. The accession of Isabella marks the end of the feudal aristocracy'.[10] This was simply not the case, but it was not until the twentieth century that historians began to revise some of the traditional judgements on Henry, Joanna and Isabella. Henry's reign is no longer considered an unmitigated failure; Joanna's legitimacy has been endorsed by several scholars and historical judgements of Isabella's achievements and innovations have been modified. Indeed, it is the view of William Phillips that 'Enrique left a set of policies and programs that his successors took over and preserved. Fernando and Isabel were merely successful in implementing them'.[11]

6 Conclusion

Why was Isabella able to secure her throne and quell the forces of disorder? What qualities did she and her husband possess which enabled them to succeed where Henry IV had so singularly failed? Part of the explanation lies with the Queen's character. She was a determined, resolute and resourceful woman, with a street-fighter's instinct for survival. Above all, she displayed strength in adversity and great personal courage. In 1477, for example, according to Pulgar she rode for three days and nights from Valladolid to Cuenca in order to persuade the military order of Santiago that it should elect her husband as its next master. Although she failed in this objective, she at least made sure that Villena was not elected and that the verdict went to a loyalist. She guaranteed privileges to nobles and town authorities, stood firmly by her promise to restore law and order and, as the only claimant with an undisputed right to the throne, behaved as if she were the Queen. The court remained principally in the north at Tordesillas and Valladolid but Isabella was already demonstrating the physical strength necessary to travel her kingdom, visiting Extremadura and Andalucía, and being welcomed by the citizens of Trujillo, Cáceres and Seville. The ceremonial handing over of the keys to the *alcázar* in Seville in July 1477, for instance, by none other than the Duke of Medina Sidonia, was a political gesture of the greatest significance. Similar ceremonies occurred at Córdoba and Toledo.

A second reason was the part played by Ferdinand. He led Isabella's troops against the Portuguese and French invasions, recaptured rebellious towns, and had an even more active itinerary than she did. Between 1475 and 1476, for example, he journeyed from Burgos to Zamora near the Portuguese border, fought the battle of Toro and captured the fortress before rejoining his wife at their first Cortes at Madrigal. His brother also aided Isabella's cause: he was given command of the Hermandad and, when his father died, neither he nor the Aragonese nobles contested the throne.

Although court chroniclers probably exaggerated the significance of the Hermandad in helping the Queen, its creation brought a rough-and-ready brand of justice to the countryside, which benefited Castilian towns as well as law-abiding landowners. The Crown had a duty to uphold law and order, and the Queen staked her reputation on accomplishing what Henry IV in his later years had failed to fulfil. *Hermandades* were not a new idea but never before had they been controlled so directly or extensively by the Crown, and by 1479 there was a notable improvement in local administration. *Corregidores* were also beginning to have an impact although they had to be used cautiously and not forced upon reluctant towns.

Finally, the failure of King Alfonso of Portugal to champion Joanna's claim to Castile proved vital in explaining Isabella's success. If he had won the battle of Toro in 1476, the situation would have been quite different but he did not; thereafter more and more Castilian nobles and towns rallied to Isabella's cause. His doubts concerning Joanna's legitimacy, the Papacy's *volte face* in revoking the dispensation allowing him to marry her, and his awareness that most Castilians actually preferred Isabella as their monarch, no doubt further weakened Alfonso's resolve. And he had enough common sense to recognise a lost cause when he saw one!

Yet, in spite of several factors which account for Isabella's success, and in particular Ferdinand's substantial contributions outlined above, Castilian chroniclers proclaimed her and her alone as the saviour of the kingdom. In his *Décadas,* for instance, Alonso de Palencia, Isabella's ambassador to Aragon in the 1470s, declared that 'if anything worthy of praise was accomplished in Andalucía, it seemed to be due to the Queen's initiative'.[12] In contrast, Ferdinand was portrayed as a procrastinator, lacking the determination necessary to take decisions. Pulgar, one of the monarchs' official chroniclers, had no doubts why the kingdom experienced such a miraculous recovery. Writing in 1485, he stated:

> 1 Evil was so deep rooted that the cure was beyond all human thought when God ... moved by mercy, gave the people as their Queen and shepherd Doña Isabel ... who married the King Don Fernando of Aragon. By her diligence and government, in a very
> 5 short time, all injustice was changed to justice, all pride to meekness, all wars and divisions ... to peace and quiet, so that the whole kingdom enjoyed security. It was certainly a marvellous thing that what many men and great lords could not agree to effect in many years, one lone woman carried out in a little time.[13]

Why did the chroniclers elevate the role of the Queen, vilify the former king and downplay her husband's contributions in the 1470s? The answer lies in the strong ties of affection between Isabella and her historians, and their readiness to distort events so as to immortalise her achievements. Of course, she possessed many virtues and was adored by her subjects. Yet if her reign was to be praised from the outset, it was necessary to exaggerate the incompetence of her predecessor, highlight the instant recovery at her accession and minimise the influence of her Aragonese husband. And this her chroniclers proceeded to do.

References
1   Fernando del Pulgar, *Crónica de los Reyes Católicos*, ed. J. de Mata Carriazo (Madrid, 1943), Cap. CV.
2   Marvin Lunenfeld, *Keepers of the City* (Cambridge University Press, 1987), p. 19.
3   Tarsicio de Azcona, *Isabel la Católica* (Madrid, 1964), pp. 430-1.

4   Lunenfeld, *The Council of the Santa Hermandad* (University of Miami Press, 1970).
5   Lunenfeld, *Hermandad*, p. 56.
6   Pulgar, *Crónica*, Cap. LXX.
7   Pulgar, *Crónica*, Cap. XXX.
8   Andrés Bernáldez, *Memorias del Reinado de los Reyes Católicos*, ed. M. Gomez-Moreno and Juan de M. Carriazo (Blass SA, Madrid, 1962), Cap. 1.
9   Pulgar, *Crónica*, Cap. XXI.
10 J.H. Mariéjol, *The Spain of Ferdinand and Isabella*, trans and ed. B. Keen (New Jersey, 1961), p. 265.
11 W.D. Phillips, *Enrique IV and the Crisis of Fifteenth Century Castile, 1425-1480* (Medieval Academy of America, Cambridge, Mass., 1978), p. 125.
12. V. Rodríguez Valencia, *Isabel la Católica en la opinión de españoles y extranjeros* (Valladolid, 1970).
13 Pulgar, *Letras, Glosa a las coplas de Mingo Revulgo*, ed. J. Domínguez Bordona (Madrid, 1929), p. 224.

Answering source-based questions on 'Securing the Throne, 1469-79'

Read the extracts from Pulgar (pages 26, 29 and 31) and Bernáldez (pages 28-9), and answer the following questions:

1   Why was the Santa Hermandad established in 1476? How useful is Pulgar's account? (5 marks)
2   How reliable is Pulgar's commentary on the restoration of law and order under Isabella in 1475? (5 marks)
3   Compare the similarities and differences of the accounts by Bernáldez and Pulgar on the nature of the Castilian civil war. (7 marks)
4   In the light of your own knowledge, how far do these extracts confirm the view that Isabella's chroniclers changed the events surrounding her accession? (8 marks)

The following points offer advice on how to answer these documentary questions.

1   The extract contains several explanations for the establishment of the Hermandad. The usefulness or value of this extract depends very much on how far you can learn something from it and so put it to use. You should consider whether it is authentic, consistent, complete and credible. Is it a typical and believable document? What can you learn from it?
2   You should discuss Pulgar's commentary in terms of its nature (the authorship, purpose of the chronicle, date and audience), assess the typicality of the views expressed, and offer analytical links to the question so as to judge the reliability of the extract in the context of

the period.

3   Comparative questions are best answered by assessing both extracts point by point in terms of their similarity and difference. Consider whether one is more complete, more useful and more reliable than the other. You should apply contextual knowledge (i.e. your knowledge of the circumstances of the time) in support of your answer.

4   You should read the extracts from Pulgar and Bernáldez and then assess their general consistency and completeness as a set using contextual knowledge to support or challenge the question. Try to give a good balance between documentary analysis and contextual evidence in reaching a judgement about the explanatory adequacy of the extracts, and indicate what the documents do *not* contain or what extra knowledge may be required.

Essay questions on this chapter appear in the study guide at the end of Chapter 3 (see pages 49-51).

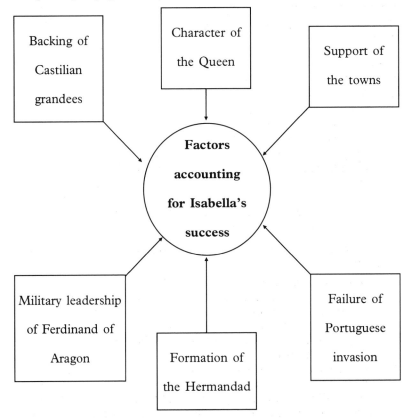

Summary - Securing the Throne, 1469-79

Government and Administration under the Catholic Monarchs, 1474-1516

The Catholic Monarchs have long been heralded as the founders of modern Spain who established a new dynasty and brought peace and good government to their war-torn kingdoms. 'The most glorious epoch in the annals of Spain', claimed W.H. Prescott in 1837. It was 'a happy golden age', wrote Ramón Menéndez Pidal in 1962. Is this praise fully justified or have historians been deceived by contemporary evidence? Do the Catholic Monarchs deserve their reputation for providing good administration or is it a myth? This chapter looks at the nature and practice of government under Isabella and Ferdinand. It considers how they ruled their kingdoms, the importance of restoring justice, and the Crown's relationship with the nobility. Finally, it examines the resurgence of aristocratic power in the course of the 1490s, the problems resulting from the succession crisis of 1504, and evidence that provincial administration was breaking down at the end of Ferdinand's reign in 1516.

1 Central Government

a) Personal Rule

In Chapter 2 we saw that, following their marriage, Isabella and Ferdinand ruled their kingdoms according to customary practice: no female was allowed to hold sovereign power in Aragon and no Aragonese ever ruled Castile. Their mutual love and readiness to share in the responsibilities of government might have given the appearance of a joint monarchy, but in fact each monarch only ruled with the other's consent. Neither sought to alter these traditional practices nor attempted to unify his or her kingdoms by building upon the dynastic unity. Indeed, upon the death of the Queen in 1504, authority in Castile passed to a regency council and Ferdinand never ruled as king.

Medieval rulers were expected to travel around their country, to meet their subjects and consult representative groups. Such journeys were often dangerous and uncomfortable, and travelling across Spain was a tiring experience. Given such difficulties, it is all the more remarkable that Isabella and Ferdinand spent so much time in transit. Every town in Castile received one or more royal visits, and some - like Burgos, Toledo and Seville - more than ten. Whenever possible they travelled together, especially if their mission was to visit a troublesome area, such as Galicia in 1486 or the war-zone in Andalucía in 1487. Both had a preference for

Castile, partly because it was the largest kingdom in the peninsula but also because it had more resources and was an altogether more rewarding country to rule. In fact, during his 37-year reign, Ferdinand spent less than four years in Catalonia, less than three in Aragon, and only six months in Valencia. Although they toured these three kingdoms together in 1481-2, showing off their newly born son, they did not return until 1487.

Of course, all royal visits helped to uphold the Crown's authority in the eyes of its subjects. As the Admiral of Castile fondly recalled in 1522, 'They knew everybody, always giving honours to those who merited them; [as they] travelled through their realms [they] were known by great and small alike'.[1] That the monarchs revisited so many towns, particularly in the first half of their reign, indicates the importance of personal monarchy in Spain and their concern to keep in close contact with the provinces. However, as long as their court remained itinerant, the establishment of a capital and centralised administration remained out of the question.

b) Conciliar Administration

The monarchs ruled their kingdoms through the royal council. In 1480 it was reorganised to direct central and local administration, oversee specialised departments of state and advise on royal affairs. Isabella appointed her most trusted archbishops and grandees to the traditional offices of Grand Chancellor, Chancellor of the Privy Seal, Constable and Admiral, and of these Diego Hurtado de Mendoza, the Archbishop of Seville and Cardinal of Spain (d. 1502), was the most influential. Meeting every working day, these royal councillors were joined by seven *letrados* (law graduates with at least ten years' experience). It was not long before real power came to rest with financial advisers, lawyers and royal secretaries, like Hernando de Zafra and Luis de Santángel. Indeed, from 1493 it was decreed that all councillors had to be *letrados* and, although grandees could continue to attend meetings, they no longer voted. There were five departments of state, dealing with foreign affairs, justice, finance, the Hermandad and the Inquisition; and they soon acquired a separate identity, each with its own administration. Two more councils later evolved: one in 1489 to supervise the military orders and a second in 1494 to administer Aragon. With the exception of the Santa Hermandad, which ended in 1498, these councils functioned throughout the period. Indeed their regular and frequent sittings gave the impression that the administration was centralised, whereas in truth the councils were *ad hoc* departments, answerable to the monarch in person, and only in the early stages of developing into a professional bureaucracy. Certainly Crown servants were much better trained and a greater number of *letrados* held posts in the Castilian administration than before, but provincial government remained in the hands of governors and viceroys, who came from the traditional aristocratic families. The Count of Tendilla, for instance, nephew of Mendoza, was governor of Granada and viceroy of Andalucía whenever the monarchs were absent from Castile, and Ferdinand's sister was viceroy of Valencia in the 1500s.

c) The Cortes

The Castilian Cortes like its counterpart in Aragon had four main functions: to vote money to the Crown, to confirm royal legislation, to offer advice when asked and to express its own grievances. It was not a regular part of the government and, as only 17 towns mainly in northern and central Castile were represented and neither the nobility nor the clergy attended, it was hardly a national assembly. As a result meetings were intermittent and usually brief. It met 16 times in all, mainly from 1498 to 1506, when political and financial crises confronted the Crown and the support of the people was urgently required. In 1498, for instance, when Isabella, the Queen's eldest daughter, suddenly died the Cortes confirmed that her infant son would be the next in line to the throne. Significantly, no Cortes met between 1482 and 1498, as Isabella relied upon the Hermandad to supply her with troops and money.

The Cortes in Aragon met more regularly. In addition to three General Cortes, when representatives from the three Aragonese kingdoms met in the same city, the realm of Aragon had seven meetings, Catalonia six, and Valencia one. It has already been noted (see pages 10-11) that these assemblies behaved more independently than their Castilian counterpart, which was a feature Ferdinand tried to change. In 1488 for example, when an argument arose in the Catalan *Diputación* (a permanent committee of the Cortes), he suspended its electoral procedure and replaced it with selection by lot whereby the names of potential candidates would be drawn from a bag. As the King now insisted on approving the names of all prospective candidates, it would appear that he was trying to increase his influence over political and perhaps financial affairs in Catalonia. If this is so, he was to be disappointed. The Aragonese Cortes similarly insisted that their grievances should always be discussed before any money was voted, and in 1515 they even refused to grant a subsidy. And in Valencia, he seems to have accepted that it was easier to receive regular customs duties from the city merchants than attempt to collect a *servicio* (financial grant) from the whole kingdom. It is not surprising that Isabella and Ferdinand came to regard their Cortes with a mixture of frustration and annoyance. Indeed, it was probably only their financial needs and their appreciation of the wisdom of regularly consulting the towns which prevented the Crown from dispensing with them altogether.

d) Town Administration

The Crown exercised variable degrees of influence over its towns. The King tried to strengthen his control in Aragon by suggesting that municipal officers should be selected by lot on the grounds that such electoral procedures would be less factious and more democratic. Names of prospective councillors were written on slips of paper, rolled into balls and dipped in wax. They were then placed in a box, shaken up and opened. When a dispute occurred in Zaragoza in 1487 its council was suspended and five years later election by lot was introduced. Similar reforms to Barcelona's council in 1498 brought more local families into city politics. This, however, was the extent of government intervention. All of the Aragonese kingdoms rejected Ferdinand's idea of sending *corregidores* (royal governors) to their towns, and he did not force the issue.

In Castile Isabella fared much better. Acknowledging that part of her success in the War of Succession (1475-79) was due to her promise to improve local government and to protect her towns' privileges from oppressive nobles, she regularly consulted her townspeople. When councils were not administered in her subjects' best interest, she intervened. In 1477, for example, she suspended Cáceres' municipal laws and ordered future officials to be appointed by lot. The towns of Trujillo in 1491 and Salamanca in 1493 received similar treatment when they were threatened by noble factions. The Crown could also influence local government by appointing *regidores* and nominating *jurados* to sit on town councils. By 1480 the number of office-holders in many towns had increased to an unmanageable size as many *regidores* handed on their posts to relatives and friends. In Córdoba, for instance, the size of the town council had risen from 24 in the fourteenth century to more than 100. The Catholic Monarchs expressed their wish to abolish hereditary office-holding and, although in practice *regidores* still nominated their successors, the overall number of councillors fell - in Córdoba's case to 44 by 1515 - and the Crown exercised more control at a local level. Parish elections could also be influenced by the Crown nominating *jurados* who were then elected by the citizens of a parish. In the opinion of John Edwards, who has studied the important Castilian town of Córdoba, by 1516 'all the major offices ... were more closely controlled by the Crown than they had been in 1474'.[2]

Long before Isabella's reign, *corregidores* had been appointed by the Crown to supervise various aspects of a town's political, social and economic life. The Queen continued this practice in the 1470s, but it was not well received. A petition of 1476, requesting that they should only be appointed with the town's consent, reflected the concern felt by some local authorities at government interference, but the Queen persisted. As she informed her Cortes in 1480, she and her husband wished 'to send *corregidores* to all cities and villages of all their kingdoms'.[3] If this had ever been seriously intended, it was impossible to achieve, although the number of towns with *corregidores* did increase from 49 to 64 by 1516. Most were appointed to Old Castile, the Cantabrian and Mediterranean coastal towns and, from 1492, to Granada. In regional towns like Bilbao, they assumed responsibility for governing the provinces as well, and in Galicia, Murcia and Granada, they complemented the work of resident governors. Yet in much of the kingdom, the *corregidores* had only a limited impact. Few towns in La Mancha and Extremadura ever saw an official, and *corregidores* had no authority to interfere in the affairs of the Hermandad, Inquisition, military orders and the Church, or in rural areas, where aristocrats and prelates exercised independent power.

At first some towns resented their presence - Murcia asked for its *corregidor* to be withdrawn in 1481 and Segovia, Burgos and Jerez all refused to accept theirs in 1483 - but on balance, local authorities saw the advantages of cooperating with the Crown. For her part, the Queen regularly complied with her towns' requests, answered their criticisms and generally enjoyed a good relationship with leading officials. However, as a study by Marvin Lunenfeld has shown, complaints against these royal officials began to grow in the 1490s.[4] Some *corregidores* stayed longer than their regulatory two years; others failed to prevent noble intimidation, and one actually persecuted residents who requested a *residencia* (an official report on his work). Most of these abuses were identified in a *pragmática* of 1500 which ordered that no *corregidor* should serve a town for more than two years, that he should not be a native of the town and that *residencias* must take place upon request.

Conditions worsened after the death of the Queen. At Burgos, the *corregidor* stayed in office for ten years, no *residencias* occurred at Medina del Campo between 1509 and 1513, nor at Toledo between 1511 and 1516, and Segovia's *corregidor* pocketed fines over a period of seven years. Well might the incoming magistrate at Medina del Campo complain that 'these kingdoms have been very badly governed and Queen Isabella, for her evil rule, was in Hell'.[5] Of course, he may have been overstating a case, but his sentiments appear sincere. Six years later, the Cortes was still complaining about poorly qualified justices, absentee officials and low standards in public administration. Thus it seems that the *corregidor* had been overworked and in many cases seriously compromised by the Crown. Peasants and urban workers believed that the *corregidor* favoured the rich and powerful, and city councils resented his interference in their affairs. Caught in the middle, he was respected by few and hated by many - a symptom as well as a cause of falling standards in local administration.

e) Justice

The monarchs inherited a judicial system that required a firm and personal hand if it was to function effectively. Ten years of civil war in both Aragon and Castile had left deep scars, and so the restoration of royal justice, contrary to the myths perpetrated by court chroniclers, would be a slow process. Both Isabella and Ferdinand dispensed justice personally. In her early years, the Queen attended public hearings every Friday in the *alcázar* and acquired a reputation for both fairness and severity. The King could be equally harsh. When Don Fernando de Velasco burned to death a group of drunken peasants because they had verbally abused him, the King defended the duke on the grounds that he had to vindicate his honour. On another occasion, when an assassin failed to stab the King to death, he ordered that his right hand should be amputated, his feet, eyes and heart removed, his flesh ripped by pincers, and his body stoned and burned as an 'example and chastisement to the rest'.[6]

Twice a week the royal council acted as a supreme court of justice. Wherever the Queen went, it followed until a permanent court of appeal (an *audiencia*), with a president and eight judges responsible for justice in the north, was established at Valladolid in 1489. There was a similar tribunal for the south of Castile in Granada, and provincial courts of lower legal status were set up at Santiago and Seville. Thus, as the reign progressed, justice by the Crown in Council was being replaced by royal judges and professional *audiencia*. At a local level, magistrates (*alcaldes*) continued to dispense the law in towns and villages, and noble and ecclesiastical jurisdictions carried on as before. The Crown could also send *corregidores* to supervise legal affairs in towns and appoint special commissioners to assist them, but they were only expected to interfere if there had been a miscarriage of justice. The majority of cases involving local people was settled by town magistrates and the appeals by *alcaldes mayores* and *corregidores*.

The most feared agent of royal justice was the Hermandad, established by Isabella as a permanent force in 1476 and subsequently expanded throughout Castile. Horse-riding archers, dressed in green and carrying the Hermandad flag bearing a golden yoke and arrows (Isabella's colours), pursued their quarry across open countryside and occasionally into towns. While a minority of offenders was guilty of capital offences like murder, rape and robbery, the most common crime was theft. Sentences, however, were cruel and summary, irrespective of the offence or status of the offender. For example, anyone convicted of stealing items valued at less than 500 *maravedís* (a labourer earned about 625 a month) was sentenced to be lashed; items valued at between 500 and 5,000 *maravedís* carried a punishment of amputation, and more expensive goods incurred the death penalty.

'At first there was much butchery', commented a royal physician, 'but it was necessary because all the kingdoms had not been pacified.' This may well have been true, and court historians were at pains to celebrate the extent to which excessive violence was quickly suppressed. Yet it remains a fact that the rural *hermandades* were very unpopular. Towns objected to high taxation levied for their upkeep and Burgos, which first requested a national militia, even refused to pay its quota in 1484. Seville and Toledo complained at the intrusion of brotherhood officials in local justice, and a subsequent law which forbade them from entering towns in search of fugitives had only limited success. Nobles, of course, resented its lack of partiality and were soon calling for its abolition. By the early 1490s the Queen agreed. Its *raison d'être* of co-ordinating troops and money, in order first to restore royal authority and then to fight the Muslims in Granada, had been fulfilled, and its council was formally dissolved in 1498. Rural *hermandades*, however, continued on a voluntary basis in Castile and the Basque provinces and taxes were still collected to fund the magistrates and archers.

Aragon had a separate legal system from Castile. Each kingdom had its own *audiencia*, which in Aragon sat in Zaragoza. There the Justiciar, assisted by two deputies and advised by five magistrates, resolved legal issues in the King's name. For much of Ferdinand's reign, the office was held by Juan de Lanuza and their relationship appears to have been very sound. Any attempt by the King to introduce reforms was smartly rebuffed. For example, when he considered introducing the Hermandad into Aragon, initially at the request of the town of Huesca in 1487, popular opposition led to its suspension within a year and its suppression in 1495. Further attempts to re-establish it were resisted by Aragonese nobles in the Cortes. No attempt was made to introduce the Hermandad into Valencia or Catalonia, and in any case the latter had its own militia known as the *Sometent*. In addition to the Christian law courts, there were Muslim courts which applied Islamic law and dealt with cases concerning *Mudéjars* in the Crown of Aragon. All *Mudéjars* were subject to the King but he refrained from interfering in their legal affairs.

2 Strengths and Limitations of the Crown

a) Crown Land and the Nobility

The key to the Crown's political strength lay in its relationship with the nobility and their mutual interest in land. Contrary to many historians' verdicts, Isabella and Ferdinand were compromised from the beginning of their reign by incompatible promises made in the 1470s. Isabella owed her throne to the support of several powerful aristocratic families, who consequently expected to be rewarded. She could not afford to undermine their authority or seize their wealth and property at will. On the other hand, the hopes of most towns were riding on her promise to protect their rights from noble incursions. To most people, this meant upholding the law and establishing a system of low and fair taxation. The Queen decided early on, however, to harness the power of the nobility to the service of the Crown.

Of course, Isabella was negotiating from a weak hand and could only hope that the nobility would remain loyal and obedient. In 1480 the Toledo Cortes agreed that she should recover all lands, gifts and hereditary pensions given away by King Henry IV between 1464 and 1474 (totalling nearly 30 million *maravedís*) but confirmed the nobles' right to land and annuities (worth more than 33 million) granted before this date. The Queen could have undoubtedly recovered more Crown property. Indeed, a strong argument can be made that once a settlement had been concluded, it would be hard for her to extract any concessions in the future. Furthermore, in granting her nobles the right to assess and collect the *alcabala* (a sales tax) and confirming their exemption from direct taxation, she was guaranteeing their economic and social supremacy, if not their political independence. Similar deals were struck by Ferdinand in his kingdoms, although he had even less to bargain with. Each of his three Cortes swore fealty to the monarchs in 1481, and the Catalan Corts voted 100,000 *libras* to compensate the nobility for the restoration of Crown land. In return the King promised to respect their privileges.

Amid these political negotiations, there were some spectacular winners and losers. Much depended upon which side a noble had been on in the civil wars and whether or not the monarchs felt he was already too powerful. Among the losers, the Marquis of Cádiz forfeited a pension worth 573,000 *maravedís* but kept control of Cádiz until he later exchanged it for a dukedom. The Marquis of Medina Sidonia agreed not to enter Seville but held on to Gibraltar until 1502, and Beltrán de la Cueva forfeited grants and pensions worth 1,400,000 *maravedís*. The Marquis of Villena, who had spear-headed the opposition to Isabella during the War of Succession, received a very fair settlement. Although he lost most of his marquisate he was allowed to retain his title and several towns including Trujillo. The Queen was probably persuaded by Villena's son-in-law, the Count of Tendilla, to treat the marquis leniently. Tendilla, a royal favourite and member of the Mendoza clan, saw the importance of preserving social stability amid this period of political change. Of course, Isabella's supporters benefited most: dukedoms were awarded to de la Cerda and Manrique, Fajardo of Murcia was allowed to keep some of the lands taken from Villena, and Cabrera, who had secured Segovia for the Queen, was given extensive properties. Of her closest allies, only Admiral Enríquez appears to have fared less well: he remained a member of the royal council but forfeited pensions worth 240,000 *maravedís*.

The notion, once widely expressed, that Isabella destroyed the Castilian aristocracy is no longer tenable. Although only five new dukedoms were created, and none after 1492, the younger sons of nobles were rewarded with the title of marquis and count, and nearly 1,000 patents of nobility had been issued by 1516. It should be noted that the monarchs were careful not to alienate Crown land and instead rewarded their subjects with newly acquired property, principally in Granada. More importantly, they continued the practice of *mayorazgo*, which settled the right of succession upon the eldest son and so preserved the unity of an inheritance (see page 54). This not only reduced friction between noble families, it went a long way towards securing aristocratic obedience to the Crown.

In practice, the nobility remained in control of regional politics: Vizcaya, for example, was dominated by the Counts of Haro and Treviño, Galicia by the Count of Lemos, and León by the Count of Luna. Some nobles continued to threaten the freedom of nearby towns, apparently with the blessing of the Crown: the Count of Benavente, for instance, controlled Valladolid, and Fajardo the port of Cartagena. Indeed, nothing better illustrates the nobles' power in the country than the number of castles built during Isabella's reign. The Crown in 1480 had ordered the demolition of rebel fortifications and forbade any new erections, but by 1504 at least 265 fortresses had been rebuilt or repaired and only 84 destroyed.[7] The *Pragmática* of 1500, which repeated the order to prohibit unlicensed castles, bears witness to the government's limited success.

Isabella and Ferdinand relied so heavily on the great families in local government that there was little they could do to suppress unlawful behaviour. Most nobles kept retainers, whereas the Crown had no standing army and only a small number of Hermandad troops, which were never enough to openly challenge a disobedient noble. In fact, many nobles themselves served in the Hermandad and the royal army raised during the 1480s and 1490s. Villena and Fonseca, for instance, commanded regiments in the Hermandad cavalry and Cifuentes and Tendilla held captaincies in the royal guards. The practice of appointing aristocrats as governors further increased their power. Such offices were hereditary and made the position of nobles like the Duke of Nájera, Viceroy of Navarre, virtually unassailable. Given these prevailing conditions, the Crown had to forge a partnership with the nobility if it was to survive: the monarchy would retain its political supremacy in central government and the nobility its social dominance in local administration.

Together they ensured the defence and stability of the country, provided, of course, that their interests did not clash. When this did occur, a great deal of patience was required by the Crown if it was to get its own way. How it gained control of the three military orders well illustrates the slow accretion of royal power. The crusading orders owned vast tracts of land, and their masters in the past had employed their wealth and armies against the Crown (see page 4). The Queen herself could not become a master but the King could. In 1477 she had failed to get Ferdinand elected to the Order of Santiago even though the Papacy had sanctioned his appointment. He had to wait more than 20 years for the incumbent to die before this happened, by which time he had also succeeded to the Orders of Calatrava and Alcántara. In each case, he had waited for the death of the master and then allowed the customary elections to run their course. As for the Orders of Montesa and St John in Aragon, they remained outside the Crown's control until Philip II's reign.

b) Royal Finances

The Crown's financial condition in 1474 was very weak. Pensions, annuities and vast tracts of Crown land had been given away, and very little revenue actually reached the Treasury. Of the 73 million *maravedís* expected, only 11 million were received. The rest had been pocketed by tax farmers or simply not collected. An enquiry early in Isabella's reign recommended three major reforms: all noble claims to lands and *mercedes* (grants made by the Crown) were to be investigated and existing rights and privileges confirmed only when they had been officially approved; a central record was to be kept; and all tax farmers were to have their accounts audited every two years. As a result, the Crown recovered nearly half of the *mercedes* collected by nobles, and its overall revenue greatly increased.

Yet, behind this notional improvement lay a different picture. Stephen Haliczer has shown in his study of the *mercedes* that it was the nobility rather than the Crown which emerged financially stronger from the investigation, and actually held more grants after the enquiry than before. Some nobles continued to collect *mercedes* to which they were not entitled, and others bribed Treasury officials and tax farmers. Furthermore, the situation worsened as the reign progressed, so that by 1516, in Haliczer's opinion, 'the reform had collapsed and the treasury reverted to a state of extreme disorganisation and confusion, with frauds of unprecedented dimensions'.[8] As most royal revenue had to be collected by tax farmers, the opportunities for corruption were obviously considerable. Indeed it seems that during the 1490s none of the duties

Crown revenue in Castile [9]			
1474	11	million	*maravedís*
1479	94	million	*maravedís*
1481	150	million	*maravedís*
1496	269	million	*maravedís*
1504	317	million	*maravedís*
1510	320	million	*maravedís*

on salt, sheep and internal customs were returned to the Treasury; that accounts were not audited accurately; and that when errors were discovered, officials ignored them. An investigation in 1497 estimated that the Crown had lost 20 million *maravedís* by fraudulent Treasury officials alone.

Ninety per cent of royal revenue came from the *alcabala,* a tax on sales, but as the clergy were exempt, the nobility collected their own payments and some towns paid a fixed sum from 1495, its real value did not significantly rise during this period. In 1504 it yielded 284 million *maravedís,* and some 300 million in 1516. The rest of the ordinary revenue came from a variety of indirect taxes on items such as salt, transport tolls and the movement of sheep. Far more significant were the special taxes granted by the Hermandad, Cortes and the Church. The Hermandad yielded an annual average of 18 million. Unlike other taxes, its collection was rigorously monitored and most of it reached the Treasurer. The Cortes was not convened for most of the 1480s and 1490s but made very valuable grants thereafter. From time to time the Church also made sizeable donations. The *cruzada,* for instance, yielded 808 million *maravedís,* principally because it was collected by district collectors, and audited and supervised by the clergy.

In spite of these extraordinary sources of revenue, the Treasury still had a shortfall, which was only made up from 1489 by loans and *juros* (10 per cent interest bearing annuities). It is ironic, although not surprising, that the largest royal creditors were aristocrats like Medinaceli, Cádiz and Aguilar. The Duke of Cádiz, for example, loaned 10 million *maravedís* in return for being given the village of Casares in Granada; and the Count of Aguilar, for so lor.g spurned by the Queen, recovered her favour and acquired the village of Montefrío for a loan of 7 million.[10] By 1516 *juros* cost the Crown in interest payments some 131 million *maravedís,* and the foundations of royal indebtedness had been laid.

Henry Kamen has suggested that the Catholic Monarchs 'survived without major financial problems'.[11] Is this really the case? They had no coherent programme, responded to difficulties with short-term measures, and failed to tackle the root cause of their problems - an inefficient, corrupt and unfair system of taxation. Moreover, a sharp rise in government expenditure on diplomacy, war and foreign affairs intensified their problems. Annual military costs rose from 20 million in 1482 to 80 million in 1504, and the Italian campaigns of 1500-4 alone cost 366 million. At the same time, the monarchs were not especially prudent in their household expenditure, or in dispensing royal patronage: between 1474 and 1504 court costs quadrupled and state pensions doubled. The Crown's finances, therefore, appeared to be stronger than they really were. Revenue had increased in the course of the reign but so too had state expenditure, and the budget could only be balanced by mortgaging future income.

c) The Death of Isabella and the Succession Crisis

The Crown's political limitations were highlighted in the early years of the sixteenth century, following the death of the Queen in 1504. The heir to the Castilian throne was Joanna, her eldest surviving but mentally unstable daughter. Isabella had no intention of allowing Joanna's husband, Philip, Archduke of Burgundy, to unite Castile and Burgundy, and nor did she intend letting Ferdinand rule both Aragon and Castile. In her will she therefore decreed that Joanna would be Queen of Castile, Ferdinand must surrender his title of King and only become the regent if Joanna was 'unwilling or unable to govern', and then only until her son, Charles (born in 1500), came of age. These instructions caused confusion. Was Castile to be ruled by Joanna, Philip, Ferdinand, or even Cisneros, the Queen's confessor? The nobility were divided over the question, city councils split into factions, and popular disturbances occurred throughout Castile, spurred on partly by severe economic conditions. In January 1505 Ferdinand duly acknowledged Joanna in the presence of the Cortes and awaited her arrival from Brussels. Speculation upon the mental health of the princess was rife and Castilian grandees like Mendoza, Benavente and Villena were already in correspondence with Philip, whom they assumed would take charge. The Constable, Admiral and both archbishops supported Joanna, and a larger if less powerful group led by Alba, Tendilla and Cifuentes gathered round Ferdinand. As one Italian diplomat shrewdly observed: 'the nobles sharpen their teeth like wild boars with the hope of a great change.'

At this delicate moment, Ferdinand married a French princess, Germaine de Foix, in October 1505. She had a claim to Navarre and any children from this union would have also had a claim to the Castilian and Aragonese thrones. Was Ferdinand making a bid to outflank his rival claimants? It is possible, and the King was noted for his devious diplomacy, but his conduct may more readily be explained by his recognition that he would never be accepted by the Castilians and that his future lay in ruling Aragon and its kingdoms. Certainly his conversations with Joanna and Philip in June 1506 did nothing to dispel this second assessment: Philip declared that he would be governing Castile in the name of his wife and that Ferdinand was no longer welcome in the kingdom. He had no recourse but to accept his lot and retire with Germaine.

Ferdinand was already en route for Naples when Philip suddenly died in September 1506. Joanna, beside herself with grief, showed all the signs of madness, and once again Castile was thrown into political chaos. The President of the Royal Council, Archbishop Cisneros, informed Ferdinand that civil disturbances were occurring throughout the country and urged him to return. In fact Castile was teetering on the brink of another civil war, as several aristocrats and nobles again threatened the country's tranquillity. Riots broke out in Ávila and Medina del Campo, and factions destabilised the councils in Valladolid, Córdoba and Toledo. The Duke of Medina Sidonia tried to recover control of Gibraltar, the Count of Lemos overran the town of Ponferrada, and the Marquis of Moya seized the *alcázar* of Segovia. At a national level, Alba, Infantado and Velasco gave their support to Ferdinand, while Nájera and Villena favoured offering the regency to Maximilian, the Holy Roman Emperor. Ferdinand returned to Castile in the summer of 1507, raised an army and confronted the rebels. Most melted away and only in Andalucía did troublesome nobles, led by the Marquis of Priego and the Count of Cabra, continue to defy the Crown. Their submission and subsequent arrest in July 1508 ended the political crisis.

Ferdinand's re-instatement as regent was confirmed by the Madrid Cortes in 1510. By then Joanna, having insisted that her husband's corpse should be taken to Tordesillas and placed in her bedroom, was bordering on insanity and considered incapable of ruling Castile. Day-to-day administration was handled by Cisneros while Aragon continued to be administered by viceroys, a state of affairs which left Ferdinand free to concentrate on foreign issues. Had his wife borne him a son (a boy died in 1509 within hours of his birth), no doubt he would have given more attention to the succession and to confronting the Castilian grandees. As it was, disaffected nobles led by Villena and Medina Sidonia, and secretly encouraged by Cisneros, sought to undermine Ferdinand's position by ingratiating themselves with the heir to the throne, Charles Habsburg, Archduke of Burgundy.

Ferdinand's health declined after 1513 and the administration was handled by Cisneros and the royal secretaries, Lope Conchillos and Francisco de los Cobos. It seems that from 1514-15 Ferdinand tried to secure the regency for his favourite, the Duke of Alba, but his attempts were in vain and Cisneros gained the support of most Castilian nobles as they jostled for offices in the new administration. Political intrigue once again characterised Castilian affairs in the closing years of Ferdinand's reign. As for the dying king, he accepted that Charles would succeed to both the kingdom of Castile and to the kingdom of Aragon. It had not been Ferdinand's intention to see Aragon ruled by a Burgundian, nor had it been Isabella's wish to see Castile united with Aragon. Yet both occurred in 1516 when Charles became the first King of Spain (see page 109).

3 How Effective were the Monarchs in Restoring the Royal Administration?

If the opinions of court writers like Pulgar, Palencia and Valera are to be believed, administration and justice were quickly restored by Isabella and the foundations of royal absolutism laid at the expense of the overmighty aristocracy. Isabella was 'the most feared and respected' Queen, declared Bernáldez; and, in the words of Pulgar, the monarchs 'administered justice to certain criminals and thieves' which 'made the citizens and farmers and all common people, who were desirous of peace, very happy'.[12] The facts seem to support this view, at least at the beginning of their reign.

At first, both Isabella and Ferdinand took a keen interest in upholding the law and disciplining overmighty nobles. The judicial apparatus was already in place and only needed enforcing. Indeed historians now recognise that in the early years of his reign, Henry IV had done just that. The country already possessed courts of appeal, which were extended by the Catholic Monarchs, and their policy of appointing more *corregidores* to resolve legal and political disputes was generally welcomed. Toledo, for instance, enjoyed a long period of domestic peace largely due to Gómez Manrique, its *corregidor*, who held in check the rival Silva and Ayala families. If a noble defied the monarchs, they dealt with him personally. In a well publicised incident in Galicia, the Count of Lemos deprived a marquis of his right to collect feudal rents, and ignored orders from magistrates and several warnings from the throne. In 1486 Isabella and Ferdinand accompanied by justices visited the province and ordered Lemos to hand over various lands, pay compensation to his complainants, and surrender the town of Ponferrada to the Crown. Lemos begrudgingly complied. Few examples exist in the 1480s of the Crown failing to enforce its will, especially when its own interest was at stake. Thus when the *alcalde mayor* of the Duke of Alba struck a royal tax collector, he was brought before the Valladolid court, and upon being found guilty, had his hand amputated and was sent into exile.

The period after 1490, however, reveals a different picture. Having secured the throne with the assistance of the nobility, the monarchs seemed in the opinion of many towns unwilling to stand up to a revival of provincial aristocratic power and even sided with the nobility in seigneurial disputes. Constable Velasco was able to threaten the villages of the Merindales in Old Castile with impunity, the Count of Salinas seized properties near to Burgos, and the Duke of Nájera in 1498 terrorised the people of Leniz with more than 1,500 soldiers. Isabella and Ferdinand had no police force or standing army, and the law offered their subjects no protection. The city of Toledo tried in vain to recover lands lost to the Count of Belalcázar and for over 20 years was frustrated at every turn: first the Crown ordered the royal council to suspend the case and then in 1511 prohibited any further appeals. Segovia similarly received short shrift from the Queen when it tried to recover town property granted to her loyal supporter Cabrera. In 1480 she had insisted that 'you make no further protest and conform yourselves with what we have ordered because if you refuse we shall be extremely angry'.[13] For the next 40 years the city tried unsuccessfully to get its claim reviewed. Even when Isabella changed her mind and revoked the grant in 1504, the Cabrera family ignored the order and continued to keep the properties.

Examples of royal bias are numerous. In a dispute over the jurisdiction of three villages between Alonso de Fonseca, captain of the royal guards, and the town of Medina del Campo in 1496, the Crown ordered the case to be transferred from the *audiencia* to the royal council to be certain that a verdict favourable to Fonseca would be reached. In the same year the Crown ordered the *audiencia* to review a case it had already heard between the city of Salamanca and the Count of Miranda, and when it seemed as if another judgement unfavourable to the count would be announced, the case was transferred to the council. Even the King was not averse to interfering in legal cases. In 1510 he informed the president of the Granada *audiencia* that he was not pleased to hear judgements awarded against his nobility and suggested that it would be helpful if judges could find some legal grounds of appeal. The law must be applied, he contended, but so must the rights of the nobility. Some nobles needed little assistance from the Crown. The Count of Aguilar, for instance, prohibited villagers who were not even his vassals from hunting in the countryside, and then successfully appealed against a judgement ordering him to stop.

The feelings of many merchants, townspeople and peasants were clearly expressed in petitions sent to the Burgos Cortes in 1512. They alleged that the judiciary was biased, many government officials were corrupt and ineffectual, and the Crown was either unable or unwilling to restrain the rich and powerful. Public confidence in the Castilian government towards the end of Ferdinand's reign therefore appears to have been very low, and in sharp contrast with official propaganda. In 1516 noble factions were as strong as ever, rebellions were breaking out in Navarre, León, and Andalucía, and aristocratic families like the Mendozas, Enríquez, Velascos and Guzmáns were in revolt.

Outbreaks of civil disorder and violence in Castile in the early years of the sixteenth century suggest that royal administration was beginning to break down. They also raise important questions for the historian. Was this lawlessness a reaction by the nobility to the death first of Isabella, then Philip, and finally Ferdinand, or did it reflect a sense of national resentment at being ruled by foreigners? Do the provincial revolts between 1506 and 1516 suggest that the Castilian aristocracy had never been effectively tamed by the Catholic Monarchs? Why did contemporary writers propagate the view that Isabella restored royal justice if it was equally evident that in the last years of her reign and for much of her husband's, there was widespread lawlessness? Did Charles V inherit a poisoned chalice? These are difficult questions to answer and, until further research has been conducted, any conclusions must be provisional. Nevertheless, it would seem reasonable to make the following propositions: firstly, many Castilians resented the prospect of being ruled by a foreigner, as they amply demonstrated in the revolt of the Comuneros against Charles V in 1519. Secondly, the Crown's relationship with the aristocracy bore a striking resemblance to that in Tudor England and Valois France. Like all medieval monarchs, Isabella and Ferdinand depended upon the consent and cooperation of their nobles in the administration of their kingdoms. Thirdly, the political achievements of the Catholic Monarchs, like those of Henry VII and Louis XI, have been exaggerated by their court propagandists and by historians - propagandists by a desire to look at the past nostalgically and historians by a readiness to accept such accounts all too uncritically.

References

1 Henry Kamen, *Spain, 1469-1714: A Society in Conflict* (Longman, Essex, 1991), p. 22.
2 John Edwards, *Christian Córdoba* (Cambridge University Press, 1982), p. 44.
3 Pulgar, *Crónica*, Cap. CXV.
4 Marvin Lunenfeld, *Keepers of the City* (Cambridge University Press, 1987).
5 Lunenfeld, *Keepers of the City*, p. 166.
6 Felipe Fernández-Armesto, *Ferdinand and Isabella* (New York, 1975), p. 117.
7 Edward Cooper, *Castillos señoriales de Castilla de los siglos xv y xvi*, vol. 1 (Fundacion Universitaria Española, Madrid, 1980), pp. 72-77.
8 Stephen Haliczer, 'The Castilian Aristocracy and the Mercedes Reform of 1478-82', *Hispanic American Historical Review*, 55 (Duke University Press, North Carolina, 1975), p. 467.
9 M.A. Ladero Quesada, *La Hacienda Real castellana en el siglo xv* (Laguna, 1973), passim.
10 Ladero Quesada, *La Hacienda*, pp. 322-24.
11 Kamen, *Spain*, p. 49.
12 Pulgar, *Crónica*, Cap. XXI.
13 General Archives in Simancas, *Cámera de Castilla*, leg. 19 n.f.

Answering essay questions on 'Securing the Throne, 1469-79' and 'Government and Administration under the Catholic Monarchs, 1474-1516'

Material from both Chapters 2 and 3 is relevant to answering questions on securing the throne and on government and administration. Questions tend to be of three main types. They can focus on the personalities of Isabella and Ferdinand, on an assessment of their achievements and limitations, or on a comparison of the Castilian and Aragonese administrations. Consider the following questions:

1 How successful was Isabella's administration of Castile, 1474-1504?
2 'Without Ferdinand, Isabella would not have secured her throne so effectively.' Do you agree?

3   To what extent and why were the administrations of Castile and Aragon dissimilar?

All of these questions are of the same basic character: they are 'evaluative', asking 'how successful' or 'to what extent'. This is obvious with 1 and 3; but 2 is of the same type. 'Without Ferdinand, Isabella would not have secured her throne so effectively', for instance, requires you to examine Ferdinand's contribution in securing the throne for Isabella and to assess it alongside other factors. Questions of this type are extremely common, and so it is worth thinking about the best way of tackling them.

Think carefully about Question 1. Logically this question, and those like it, can be answered in three different ways: you can say that Isabella's administration was 100 per cent successful, that it was 100 per cent unsuccessful, or you can opt for some in-between position, arguing that it was partly successful and therefore partly unsuccessful. It is always worth at least considering the 'extreme' positions: after all, a 100 per cent answer will have the virtues of being clear-cut and definite. Most often, however, since history is rarely black-and-white, you will probably go for some sort of middle position. To say that it was 'partly successful' will not be definite or ambitious enough. What other, more precise, form of words might be used? Obviously this depends on how successful you think Isabella was. If there are, in your opinion, only minor and relatively unimportant issues on which she did not succeed, you might perhaps choose the word 'overwhelmingly' to qualify 'successful'. If, on the other hand, you think that successes and failures are even in number and importance, you might choose another term, such as 'balanced' or even 'fifty-fifty'. It does not matter what words you choose so long as their meaning is clear and so long as they fit your interpretation of events: do not be led astray, into an untenable argument, by an ill-judged choice of terminology.

Once you have decided on how to interpret this question and you are satisfied that you have acquired enough evidence to support your argument, put your ideas on paper in an essay plan. This can be done point by point or diagrammatically. Experiment to see which method you prefer. Which sections of Chapters 2 and 3 are most useful? You will need to think critically at this stage to ensure that your approach is relevant and coherent. It may help if you number your points in order of importance; this will enable you to begin with the most significant idea and to work logically through your list when you write your essay. It cannot be emphasised too much that the key to a successful essay is the first paragraph. Never just plunge into an essay and write about the topic: instead you must answer the precise question that has been set, and in the first paragraph you should be reassuring the examiner that you have thought about the question and are answering it directly and relevantly. Hence in the first paragraph of an answer to Question 1 you would do three things. First, you would define the terms of the question (especially 'successful'); next, you would break the topic down into smaller sub-divisions, on each of which you would subsequently have a whole paragraph; and, finally, you would outline an argument - and for Question 1 this means generalising about the extent to which Isabella's administration was successful (and, therefore, the degree to which it was unsuccessful). This will probably involve balancing Isabella's successes against her failures, but do not be afraid to conclude that some aspects of her policies were neither successes nor failures. Alternatively, you might perhaps adopt the judgement that her policies were short-term successes and long-term failures. In fact the arguments/interpretations that could be given are endless. All that is important is that you do have a relevant argument and that you can support it with evidence. At the end of the essay, in the concluding paragraph, return once again to the central issue - the extent of success/failure - and hammer home your view. Often you might choose to use forms of words such as 'on the one hand' (followed by a brief rehearsal of the arguments for that view) and 'on the other hand' (followed by evidence for the opposing interpretation), ending with as exact a conclusion as you can formulate.

Examine Questions 2 and 3. What terms would you need to define at the outset of each essay? How could you break down the relevant factual material into coherent sub-divisions? And what form of words would you choose to express your view about the evaluative issues asked in the questions? Which sections in Chapters 2 and 3 are particularly relevant? Your practice on these questions, and those given later in this book, should enable you to tackle unseen questions of this type with real confidence.

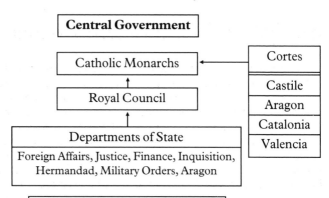

Central Government

	Cortes
Catholic Monarchs ←	Castile
↑	Aragon
Royal Council	Catalonia
↑	Valencia
Departments of State	
Foreign Affairs, Justice, Finance, Inquisition, Hermandad, Military Orders, Aragon	

Administering the Kingdoms

		Castile	Aragon	Catalonia	Valencia
PROVINCES		Catholic Monarchs ↑ Royal Council and its departments	Viceroy and Council	Viceroy and Council	Viceroy and Council
			↑ Justiciar	↑ *Diputación*	
		↑ Governors			↑
TOWNS		↑ *Corregidores* ↑ *Regidores* and *Alcaldes*	*Regidores* and *Alcaldes*	*Regidores* and *Alcaldes*	*Regidores* and *Alcaldes*

Justice

		Castile	Aragon	Catalonia	Valencia
CORREGIDORES		Queen/Viceroy	King/Viceroy	King/Viceroy	King/Viceroy
		↑ Council	↑ Council/Justiciar	↑ Council	↑ Council
		↑ *Audiencia*	↑ *Audiencia*	↑ *Audiencia*	↑ *Audiencia*
		Alcaldes Hermandades	*Alcaldes*	*Alcaldes Sometent*	*Alcaldes*

Summary - Government and Administration under the Catholic Monarchs, 1474-1516

CHAPTER 4

Social and Economic Issues

In this chapter we examine the main social and economic developments of this period. The Crown and the nobility shared a number of cultural and economic interests, not least a passion for building palaces and churches. Merchants and townspeople saw an increase in trade, and both Castilian and Catalonian peasantry enjoyed comparatively stable living conditions after several years of political and social distress. Yet, amid this era of apparent prosperity, a dual economy was developing within both the peninsula as a whole and Castile. Agriculture and industry were falling behind trade and commerce through lack of investment, the Crown's interests often overrode regional and local considerations, and the economic wealth of the country was becoming more and more concentrated in the south-west of Castile. As you study this chapter, you should assess the social and economic policies of the Catholic Monarchs before deciding how far Spanish society changed during their reign and whether they left their kingdoms in a stronger or weaker condition economically.

1 Society

a) The Crown and Nobility

There was no permanent court in fifteenth-century Castile to which the Crown could attract a resident nobility, dispense its patronage or develop a distinctive culture. The Catholic Monarchs, however, displayed sufficient interest in humanism, education and architecture to stimulate some of their subjects into patronising the Arts. Isabella owned some 400 books, most of which were of a religious nature; she enjoyed dancing and music, and employed a chapel choir which travelled with the court. As a patron of several poets, scholars and writers, she played an important part in helping to develop a more cultured society. The printing press, which had been introduced into Spain in 1473, also helped to raise levels of literacy. By 1500 some 25 towns had presses. It is interesting to note that Isabella, who wrote and studied Latin, promoted the language not simply because of its literary merits but as a means of raising the standard of future judicial, administrative and ecclesiastical office-holders. She invited Peter Martyr, the celebrated Italian scholar, to visit Castile with the explicit purpose of educating the nobility.

Nobles who chose to receive Latin instruction usually did so through private tutors, whereas most young men of noble blood attended one of the many town grammar schools founded at this time. Even a small amount of Latin was enough to open doors to an attractive career in the royal service. As a result, great kudos was placed on attaining a law degree and the best administrative and legal positions went to the *letrados*, law graduates with at least ten years' experience who usually held two degrees. There were thousands of offices in the Castilian and Aragonese administration and, as the bureaucracy expanded, so too did opportunities for employment. The creation of new colleges in Valladolid and two new universities at Alcalá (1508) and Cuenca (1510), were specifically designed to encourage more mature students to take advanced degrees, and helped boost the large numbers of legally trained graduates. The Catholic Monarchs were the first in Spain to regulate the quality of university education: they introduced state funding and determined the content of the curriculum, entrance requirements and assessment procedures.

Only a few nobles went to university but many, no doubt influenced by the Queen, developed an interest in cultural pursuits, especially the building of palaces, churches and schools. The 'Isabelline' style of architecture was based on Flemish and Gothic designs and became a favourite with several noble families who converted their castles into palaces (and occasionally their palaces into fortresses!). The Palacio del Infantado, the home of the Mendoza in Guadalajara, the Hospital of St Sebastian in Córdoba, and the Medinaceli's palace in Cogulludo, with their rectangular walls, interior courtyards and gardens, circular towers and floors two or three storeys high supported by fluted columns, were built in this style. A minority of Castilian nobles, like the Count of Tendilla, preferred the Italian classical designs and commissioned monasteries and libraries in this Renaissance style.

The Catholic Monarchs saw the advantages of channelling the nobles' energy and money into building projects: it encouraged feelings of creativity and preservation rather than wanton destruction, which had typified the civil war period, and it helped to reinforce the political stability which the Crown was so keen to maintain. The previous chapter demonstrated how the land settlement of 1480 had helped to restore royal authority and pacify the nobility. This relationship between the Crown and the aristocracy was central to the development of medieval Spanish society. Political appointments rested with the Crown and preferment went to those nobles who were loyal, cooperative and worthy of reward. Social pre-eminence, however, was judged by the size and value of property and their entitlement. The Catholic Monarchs created few hereditary titles but when they did, titles such as count, marquis and duke conferred social as well as political status. According to customary Spanish law, younger children were entitled to a 'fair' inheritance, but the Cortes confirmed in 1505 that the right of entail would pass to the eldest son, and thus nobles' estates and the titles which accompanied them would remain in their family and their economic condition would be rendered reasonably stable.

The Catholic Monarchs continued the practice of granting *señorios* (lordships which carried jurisdiction over an area) to the nobility, partly in recognition of acts of loyalty and service but also as a means of exercising political power over them. The nobles realised the attraction of *señorios:* they yielded handsome rents and feudal dues; good agricultural land might provide wool, wine, honey and olives; some properties contained mines, mills and presses; others commanded the right to levy tolls on roads, bridges and rivers. In this way the Marquis of Villena derived much of his wealth from sheep farming in Murcia, the Count of Haro from collecting customs duties along the Cantabrian coast, and the Count of Benavente rents from his fair at Villalón.

The late fifteenth century saw noble families not only take a close interest in the management of their estates but also in the welfare of their vassals. In the Crown of Aragon, Ferdinand preserved the traditional privileges granted to his own vassals and defended them from the incursions of particularly assertive nobles. In Castile some lords claimed that they should be exempted from taxation and encouraged immigrant labour from nearby villages to settle on their estates. The inevitable outcome was an increase in litigation in both Aragon and Castile between towns and landowners over rival claims to control villages and their inhabitants, especially in the 1490s (see page 47). The Valencian towns of Játiva, Alcira and Murviedo were in regular conflict with surrounding lordships, and in Castile during this decade the towns of Cuenca, Soria and Segovia were all in dispute with local nobles about high transit duties, bridge tolls and land rights. Of course, the nobility knew that what the Crown could grant, it could also withhold and in extreme circumstances take away, although this appears to have rarely happened. Not every noble family indulged in economic activities or imposed financial and social obligations upon local towns and villages near to their estates, but many, like the Santillana and Infantado branches of the Mendoza family, most certainly did. Through skilful exploitation of their economic and social rights as one of the country's largest estate owners, courtesy of their favoured political status, the Mendoza had become 'by far the wealthiest noble house in Castile'.[1]

b) The Peasantry

Only a small number of nobles derived their livelihood from trade, sheep farming and industry. Most were totally dependent on collecting rents from the thousands of peasants and labourers who worked their land. A low rate of inflation and a small but rising population ensured that in Castile wage levels rose faster than food prices, so conditions for most peasants were not oppressive. Agrarian disturbances did occur in Galicia in 1478-80 but they appear to have been inspired more by political than social or economic issues and were confined to that province. Reasonably good harvests, at least until the turn of the century, increasing political stability and the opportunities for work, may well account for the apparent absence of peasant uprisings during this period. Similar trends were evident in Aragon and Valencia at this time. When tension did arise, in the 1490s for instance, it was often a result of landowners encroaching upon peasants' grazing and farming rights, and litigation rather than violence appears to have followed.

The condition of the peasantry in Catalonia was quite different. In spite of receiving assurances from Ferdinand that in the aftermath of the civil war (1462-72), they would be freed from the 'five uses' (onerous feudal obligations), nothing had been done. A rebellion in 1484-5 convinced him that action had to be taken and resulted in his Sentence of Guadalupe in the following year. The *remensa* peasantry, who had been subject to the 'five uses', were released from their feudal obligations and allowed to sell their produce, and the Crown, Church and nobility were granted 67,000 *libras* in compensation. This settlement has been regarded by historians as a compromise which favoured the landed groups, but the Catalonian peasantry appears to have been satisfied and remained peaceful subjects despite suffering from poor economic conditions in the early sixteenth century.

c) Urban Groups

Population levels in Spain began to rise in the second half of the fifteenth century. Intermittent outbreaks of plague - the city of Valencia had an epidemic in 1489 and Barcelona in 1490 - had little impact and did not deter the steady movement of labour from the countryside to the towns. Most people still worked on the land but urban population levels appear to have been rising particularly in Seville, Toledo, Barcelona, Zaragoza and Valencia.

Of these cities, Seville was growing most rapidly. By 1516, it was the largest city in Castile, and by the middle of the sixteenth century it would surpass Valencia. It owed its growth to its trading and commercial monopoly with America. The wealth this trade generated encouraged merchants, artisans and financiers, as well as thousands of poor people to settle there. More is known about this city than any other in early modern Spain, thanks mainly to the large collections of family and public documents which have survived and been studied by historians in recent years. It is apparent that great magnates like the Duke of Medina Sidonia and Luis Ponce de León owned ships and profited from the carrying trade, and that a large number of merchants involved in the transatlantic trade were of Jewish origin. Pedro del Alcázar, for instance, imported grain and farmed the customs duties of Seville, and Antón Bernal and Juan de Córdoba invested in the shipment of goods and slaves and then offered loans at remunerative rates of interest to fellow traders. Genoese merchants - some of them bankers, some traders - were also well established in the city. Without the financial backing of Francisco Pinelo, Columbus might not have embarked on his first two voyages to America. And, as a result of his success, more Italian families emigrated to Seville in the last decade of the fifteenth century to take advantage of trading opportunities with the New World. Of some 61 Sevillian trades and professions listed in a survey of 1510, the most important were goldsmiths, silversmiths, pharmacists, mercers, grocers, shoemakers, clothiers, leather workers, carpenters and masons. Many of them sold goods to America but most of their trade was with the domestic market.

A similar picture is evident in most Iberian towns although drawn on a smaller scale. Merchants, artisans and professional groups served their home town and immediate localities; few conducted business overseas but the opportunities for social and economic advancement were improving for the educated, skilled and industrious groups.

The urban poor were less fortunate. The number of beggars and vagrants in Spanish towns appears to have increased during the reign of the Catholic Monarchs, but the Crown did little to tackle the problem. No new legislation was passed, and existing laws, which dated from the thirteenth century, do not seem to have been strictly enforced. The 1490s, nevertheless, did see some acts of private and public charity. Córdoba, for instance, saw four new hospitals including a house for 33 poor women founded by Doña María de Sotomayor in 1496. Cardinal Pedro Mendoza provided money in his will to amalgamate several small hospitals in Toledo into one large institution and, after much delay, the Hospital of Santa Cruz opened in 1514. There were also a small number of royal foundations. The Crown established a general hospital for pilgrims, pauper children, and the sick and infirm in Santiago de Compostela, a hospital for old and injured soldiers in Seville, and syphilis hospitals in Granada and Toledo. Many towns had a San Lázaros or leper house, usually situated outside the walls. In 1477 the Crown appointed two officials specifically to supervise the confinement of lepers to such houses, but it seems that this decree was not always enforced. Moreover, by the end of the reign there was widespread feeling that many hospitals were inefficiently administered, funds were misspent and patients neglected, and little had been done to remedy these complaints. Indeed, a request to deal with the problem of vagrancy and the poor was raised at Charles V's first Cortes.

2 Economic Issues

a) Government Policies

Isabella and Ferdinand took a close interest in shaping the economic welfare of their kingdoms and introduced a number of reforms. Some historians, like Stephen Haliczer, have likened their policies to a crude form of mercantilism in which the state intervened to regulate and protect native trades and industries and tried to control bullion supplies.[2] Thus the export of gold and silver was prohibited, *consulados* (boards of trade) were set up, navigation laws attempted to promote the shipbuilding industry, Seville was given the monopoly of all trade and commerce with America, and royal ordinances of 1494 and 1511 sought to raise the quality of cloth manufacture throughout the kingdom. There was a similar picture of state intervention in Catalonia. The Cortes passed a law in 1481 to protect the coral and textile industries, and import duties were imposed on French cloth in 1498.

Yet Haliczer and the economic historian Jaime Vicens Vives have also commented upon the inconsistent, piecemeal and at times contradictory policies of this era. The Catholic Monarchs gave some guilds like the Carters and the Mesta extensive privileges while other companies were more closely supervised. Non-Castilians were prohibited from trading with America in spite of the obvious advantages such trade would have brought to the eastern kingdoms and no attempt was made to remove the tolls on bridges, ports and frontiers, which stifled trade between and within the Spanish kingdoms. In fact, the government policy, if indeed it may be so called, was to treat each kingdom as a separate economic unit and to allow the regional economies to flourish with the minimum of state interference. Only one reform achieved a degree of economic union: this was when the currency of each kingdom was standardised in 1497. It seems likely, therefore, that no economic integration occurred precisely because, in the opinion of Vives, 'Ferdinand and Isabella did not in fact aspire to the attainment of an effective unity in Spain'.[3] The unification of the kingdom was not a realistic objective, and in any case the economic welfare of the country was always of secondary importance, especially if it clashed with political or religious considerations.

b) Agriculture

How best to feed a growing population in adverse conditions and with limited resources was a recurring problem for towns and cities alike in early modern Spain. Poor soil, unreliable supplies of water, primitive farming methods and little fertile land - these were difficulties common to both Castile and Aragon. How best to maximise revenue from the millions of migratory sheep controlled by the Mesta and even larger non-migratory flocks was the Crown's principal concern. Wool was the basis of Castilian trade, and taxes on sheep and wool were an important source of revenue. Arable and pastoral farming were not mutually exclusive, but there is little doubt that the Catholic Monarchs did nothing to weaken the sheep farmers and particularly favoured the Mesta.

At the outset it was declared that any enclosures established in Henry IV's reign must be destroyed; taxes levied on landowners since 1464 on royal sheepwalks were annulled; and all common land returned to pasture. A decree of 1489 further confirmed the four main *cañadas* - the

Leónese, Segovian, Sorian and Manchegan sheepwalks - and ordered the expulsion of farmers who had encroached on Mesta property. The appointment of a royal councillor as its president in 1500 was ample proof of its prestige. In the following year sheep farmers received new privileges which allowed them access to any fields where sheep had once grazed and granted them rents at very low rates. Henry Kamen believes that, in spite of its considerable power, the Mesta did not abuse its authority and was mindful of the effects it could have upon arable and cattle farming, vineyards and fruit farms. In his view, arable farmers did not suffer.[4] Contemporaries were not so certain. The town of Segovia, for instance, was frequently in litigation with the Mesta in the 1490s. Local herdsmen, denied the right to enclose or have access to common pasturage but obliged to let sheep farmers onto their land, frequently clashed with royal magistrates, who invariably found in favour of the Mesta. Of course, disagreements over enclosures not only concerned the Mesta. The nobility also increased their properties at the expense of commoners, and, as principal members of town councils, often thwarted attempts to restore pasture to arable.

There were serious food shortages throughout Spain after 1504. These could have been caused by sheep farmers overstocking the commons, inadequate agricultural techniques or the inability of farmers to meet the needs of an expanding domestic market, but a series of poor harvests over a five year period was most likely to blame. In good years Andalucían farmers exported wheat, but even they found themselves having to import it after 1506. Government efforts to control the price of grain by imposing a duty known as a *tasa* in 1502 proved unworkable and may have discouraged farmers from selling their crops, and so accentuated the food shortage. Moreover, the plague of 1506-7 was so severe that it was still remembered by Castilians more than 70 years later. The opening of public granaries in Seville and other cities brought only limited relief. Indeed, in times of dearth each region looked to its own devices for survival and neither expected nor received any state assistance. The Catholic Monarchs, it can be argued, did what they could to modernise agricultural methods, but farmers were reluctant to change. In 1494, for example, it was suggested that soil fertility would improve if they turned from a two to a three-field system but the idea of leaving two fields fallow instead of one and letting sheep manure them proved unattractive.

The situation in the Crown of Aragon was little better. Food shortages in 1484 and 1503 produced famine in Valencia, and wheat was regularly imported from Sicily and Sardinia. Little grain now came from Majorca, whose economy continued to decline; and Catalonia, denied access to the markets of Castile, depended on subsistence farming. One interesting feature of the Aragonese kingdoms was their farmers' attitude towards sheep: they were not accorded privileged status. Thus in 1511, the Monzon Cortes prohibited the passage of flocks through cultivated lands, a measure that would have been unthinkable in Castile.

c) Trade and Commerce

Trade and commerce dominated local economies. Central and northern Castile were areas of considerable activity but lagged behind the more fertile region of Andalucía in the south and the port of Seville. This had the highest volume of customs duties, trading in northern Europe, Africa, the Mediterranean and, in the early sixteenth century, the Atlantic. The greatest expansion came in transatlantic trade. Total shipping sailing between Seville and America rose from 300 *toneladas* in 1504 to more than 5,000 in 1516.[5] In 1503 the city was granted the sole right to handle all trade and commerce with the New World and a *consulado*, known as the *Casa de Contratación*, was established to administer it. As a result, goods and merchants arrived from all over Castile and the city's wealth rapidly increased. Other commercially driven towns like Toledo, Valladolid, Ávila, and Medina del Campo, were drawn more and more towards Seville and the New World which beckoned beyond the horizon.

Until the discovery of America, most of these towns traded in wool and regarded Burgos in the north of Castile as the centre of distribution. They had little contact with Seville. Trade in Burgos had been subject to local control for some years, but in 1494 the Crown formally granted it a *consulado*, thus confirming it as the kingdom's premier woollen town. Its authority included shipping contracts, marine insurance and setting the sailing dates of merchant fleets leaving the northern ports. Bilbao, one of Burgos's principal ports, also received its own *consulado* in 1511, whereby shipping and freight transport were brought under its control. For a few years relations between the two towns were inevitably hostile.

The idea of *consulados* was introduced into Castile by Ferdinand, who had seen them operate successfully in Valencia and Barcelona. He believed that the appointment of a board of directors to regulate a trade, administer its affairs and resolve all legal issues would serve everyone's best interests. Similar reasoning lay behind his introduction of guilds into Castile. They had been long established in Catalonia, where he saw the advantages of setting out rules governing apprenticeships: the standard of work would rise and sales would increase. What he did not anticipate was the opposition from Castilian workers to this piece of state intervention. Hitherto, craft and trade associations had been founded on charitable and religious principles; Ferdinand's innovation was quite different and was seen as an attempt by the government to restrict their freedom to work when, where and how they liked. Not surprisingly some historians have argued that personal initiative was repressed and economic progress in Castile was hindered rather than advanced.

Further obstacles to the expansion of domestic trade were the proliferation of tolls and poor inland transport. The problems were interrelated. Tolls were levied to raise money to maintain the roads, rivers and bridges, but many of the taxes were collected by nobles who pocketed the duties; and, as the Crown had no wish to cause trouble, questions were not asked if the money was put to other uses. In 1480 the Toledo Cortes prohibited all transit taxes introduced since 1464 in an attempt to lower costs to merchants and local traders. This measure had little effect because older transport taxes remained, and in 1497 the Carters guild, one of the kingdom's most extensive road users, was granted exemption from all traffic taxes. Three years later, the government made all local guilds responsible for the maintenance of communications in their locality, but there was rarely sufficient money available to repair the highways or build new roads. An enquiry of 1511 was not untypical in revealing that the roads in Cantabria were in a very poor condition and twelve bridges between Laredo and Aguera had been swept away and not rebuilt.

Merchants also had to pay tolls when they entered and left the kingdoms. Royal customs officers operated at each of the internal frontiers and maritime ports, and only along the Castilian-Portuguese border did trade move freely. In the coastal towns and along the inland borders between Navarre, Aragon and Castile, tax farmers collected customs duties. This lack of economic cooperation between the kingdoms, a legacy of their political history, further reduced the volume of trade and, of course, perpetuated feelings of separatism.

One important reform occurred in 1497 and represented the Crown's only major attempt at economic integration. 'If, in reality, Castile was a series of regions and "markets" rather than a cohesive economic unit', writes Angus Mackay, 'the monetary, minting, and governmental systems still played a co-ordinating role which imposed a "nominal" unity on the kingdom.'[6] A *pragmática* declared that the Castilian gold ducat, the Valencian gold excelente and the Catalonian gold principat would all be worth 375 *maravedís*. Note that the gold double excelente (see page 62) bore the heads of the Catholic Monarchs; the reverse carried increasingly elaborate coats of arms of their dynasty.

Although each kingdom continued to mint its own coinage, the production of a single coin, acknowledged by all the kingdoms, went some way towards ending the disparity in their rates of exchange and, in turn, stimulated trade between the kingdoms. Indeed, the Catholic Monarchs' fiscal policy was consistently sound. One of Isabella's pledges before she became Queen was that she would restore the currency and with it her merchants' confidence to trade with Castilian coins. It would also guarantee the value of pensions and annuities, which was what mattered to the nobility. King Henry IV actually began restorative action in 1473 by ordering the six royal mints to issue coins of enhanced silver content, and so stabilise the *maravedí*. Other illegal minting houses, however, continued to operate and must have caused confusion, but at least the Catholic Monarchs recognised the importance of a stable currency. They upgraded coins throughout their rule and never resorted to a policy of debasement. This had been a feature of the 1460s and had been a principal cause of inflation.

The three most important overseas markets for Spanish trade were northern Europe, Italy and America. Bruges in the Netherlands was Castile's main base for its woollen exports, although agents also resided in France, England and Germany. Wine, iron and leather goods were also exported. Ferdinand adopted a bullish strategy in trying to revive the flagging trade in his eastern kingdoms. Sardinia and Sicily, both Aragonese islands, were forced to take only Catalonian cloth, Genoese and French shipping was banned from using Catalonian and Valencian ports, and markets were expanded in Naples and established in north

Photo of a gold double excelente

Africa, Egypt and Rhodes. As a result, Barcelona's overseas trade recovered, and with it the financial and economic stability of Catalonia. Valencia and Aragon fared less well. Neither conducted much overseas trade, and Valencia, which had eclipsed Barcelona in the second half of the fifteenth century, fell away again. Exclusion from the lucrative American market cannot have helped its economy flourish in an increasingly competitive world.

As already noted, Andalucía's trade with the New World enabled its merchants to export native food and goods. Olives, wheat, ceramics and leather materials all made their way across the Atlantic. In return, the *Casa de Contratación* received gold bullion in ever-increasing amounts. The Spanish Crown was entitled to one-fifth of the total; merchants and investors took the remainder. There can be little doubt that, as the volume of gold entering Seville increased and then passed into the domestic and continental economies, inflationary trends must have been stimulated. One writer in 1513 commented: 'Today a pound of mutton costs as much as a whole sheep used to'[7], but the full effects would not be felt until the reign of Charles V.

d) Industry

The development of Spanish industry took second place to trade and commerce. Traditional industries like Toledan leather, Sevillian soap, Vizcayan iron and shipbuilding in Barcelona continued to grow, but silk and textile production underwent a decline largely as a result of government policies. The principal supplier of silk was Granada, where the Muslims produced it for sale in Murcia and Andalucía. The conquest of the province in 1492 and subsequent persecution of *Mudéjars* saw production levels fall, as many skilled workers left the region. By 1503, in spite of an influx of immigrant Christian settlers, the

	Crown	Private	Total
1503-5	43.7 million	123.2 million	166.9 million
1506-10	96.2 million	271.1 million	367.3 million
1511-15	140.9 million	397.0 million	537.9 million

The amount of gold bullion (in maravedís) *entering Seville*[8]

production of Granadan silk was in sharp decline.

The cloth industry was adversely affected in two ways. First, Isabella was intent upon removing the Jews from Castile and encouraged the Inquisition to investigate the *Conversos*. According to Pulgar, when Isabella was informed of the adverse effect the inquisitorial campaign against the *Conversos* of Andalucía was having on the region's economy in the 1480s, 'setting little importance on the decline of her revenue, and prizing highly the purity of her lands, she said the essential thing was to cleanse the country of that sin of heresy'.[9] The Jews were skilled artisans, wealthy merchants and indispensable investors, so the emigration of between 80,000 and 100,000 in the 1490s was a serious blow to the textile industry.[10] Second, a decision was taken in 1494 to stop the production of cheap woollen cloth in favour of more expensive material. The main beneficiaries were towns in southern Castile like Seville, Córdoba and Murcia, where high-grade white merino wool was either exported or processed into cloth for the domestic and Flemish market. It was understood that at least one-third of all wool had to be sold locally but this was not always adhered to by woollen merchants. In this respect the northern cloth towns suffered most. The quality of their locally produced wool had never been very good, but at least it was cheap and more than served the needs of local markets. Now traders were obliged to buy more expensive foreign material and sheep owners, eager to maintain their profits, began to sell their wool directly to woollen merchants for export rather than for home consumption. As a result, unemployment levels began to rise in textile towns like Burgos, Madrid and Cuenca. In 1507 Segovian merchants complained of wool shortages, high prices and rising unemployment. Cuenca cloth manufacturers in 1514 protested that Genoese wool merchants were buying up and exporting nearly all of the wool and in 1516 Burgos merchants called for a prohibition of wool exports locally and a ban on foreign woollen cloth. In retrospect, the government's aim to increase cloth exports only benefited a small number of towns, some of which were already among the most prosperous in Castile; the northern towns needed every assistance they could get from the state but instead experienced an industrial decline and an increase in unemployment.

3 Assessment

How far did Spanish society change during this period? The diversity of Spanish culture has already been remarked upon and this continued to be the case in the late fifteenth century. An interest in the Italian and Burgundian renaissances, the growth of humanism and the study of Latin, and the introduction of the printing press all helped to produce a better educated and more sophisticated nobility. Having secured their family estates, they increasingly sought to transform their fortified castles into residential palaces. The emergence of *letrados* was a further demonstration of the value of a classical education. Most Castilian and Aragonese peasantry also enjoyed a period of comparative prosperity. Wages were rising, prices were stable and there was adequate work in the countryside, at least until the second decade of the sixteenth century. In Catalonia, the *remensa* peasants had gained their freedom and agrarian conditions were not oppressive. Town life was changing rapidly. Castilian merchants and professional groups saw a dramatic increase in trade and commerce, which led to a growth in business and rising prosperity for those in work. The urban poor, however, were not in a position to benefit from the new commercial opportunities. As the level of population began to rise, town authorities were faced with the problem of vagrancy, a problem which would continue to grow in the sixteenth century.

Did the Catholic Monarchs leave the economy in a stronger condition than at their accession? It is apparent that they intended to enhance the welfare of their subjects and, in several cases, succeeded. First, Castile's economy still depended heavily on the wool trade; high quality wool remained in demand in the Low Countries and Castile had plenty of it. The Catholic Monarchs protected the Mesta's monopoly and, from the Crown's perspective, it would have been foolish to do otherwise. Taxes on wool and sheep were easy to collect, lucrative and guaranteed. Second, the establishment of trade links with America and the unforeseen windfall of gold bullion proved extremely beneficial. Opportunities for Spanish industry, trade and commerce to expand seemed endless and the government stood on the threshold of acquiring unimaginable treasure, although it would need careful handling if it were not to be wasted. Third, the Crown's currency policy was very sensible. By maintaining the quality of Castile's coinage and establishing a currency common to each of its kingdoms, the Crown created the means of achieving monetary if not economic union. Moreover, as their gold currency was based on the Venetian ducat and Venice commanded universal respect in mercantile circles, their overseas trade was also strengthened. Finally, the financial status and prosperity of Barcelona recovered from the effects of its civil war in the 1460s. Trade and agriculture improved, along with peasant-landlord relations, and links with Mediterranean and Italian merchants were also renewed.

It is evident in the last quarter of the fifteenth century that several European rulers recognised the advantages which trade could bring and introduced an elementary form of protectionism to their country's economy. Louis XI, for example, regulated the quality of French cloth, linen and silk production; Henry VII passed navigation laws to encourage the export of goods in English ships; and John II of Portugal sought to establish a monopoly of European trade with west and south Africa. We have already seen that the Catholic Monarchs pursued similar policies. But it is clear that the Spanish economy had a number of weaknesses - poor communications; a network of internal customs duties and inland tolls; and resistance to state intervention in effecting changes in agriculture, guilds and industry. While it is true that such difficulties existed in most west European states at this time, the Spanish Crown was at fault in four respects.

First, it failed to promote native industries and relied too much on exporting raw wool instead of developing its own textile industry. Insufficient assistance was given to investing in the wine, ceramics, iron and shipbuilding industries; and where state subsidies were available, they were often inappropriately targeted. For instance, more merchant ships were needed if Spain was to break the Italian carrying cartel, but shipwrights only received a grant if they built ships of 600 tons or more. As this was three times the size needed to cross the Atlantic, the Crown was either trying to create a navy rather than a merchant marine or it had been wrongly advised as to how best to implement its own navigation acts.

Second, Isabella always put religious considerations ahead of economic. The expulsion of Jews and Muslims, and the dispersal of *Conversos* and *Mudéjars,* especially in Castile, had an adverse effect on the silk, leather and textile industries. Isabella particularly believed that economic sacrifices were justified in the name of Christianity. Although Ferdinand concurred in his treatment of the Jews, he was far more tolerant towards the *Mudéjars* in his kingdoms (see Chapter 5).

Third, the decision to grant total control of American trade and commerce to the *Casa de Contratación* in Seville, and to deny the eastern kingdoms any access to this market, was a serious mistake. It deepened regional economic differences within Castile and intensified hostility between the Spanish kingdoms. Many Catalans and Valencians were understandably concerned that as more and more bullion entered Seville, inflation would spread through the peninsula and the value of their own currency would decline.

Finally, by encouraging foreign merchants, especially the Genoese, to finance and supervise vital aspects of the transatlantic trade, the Crown failed to protect native trades and industries. It may have been difficult to persuade Spanish nobles and merchants to finance voyages and speculate their money in risky enterprises but it was surely not impossible, especially if the Catholic Monarchs had been genuinely mercantilistic. A number of nobles and Sevillian merchants did invest in the early expeditions to the New World. In this respect, the observation in 1512 by Francesco Guicciardini, the Florentine ambassador to Castile, that 'Spaniards do not dedicate themselves to trade because they consider it dishonourable', seems less than fair. Nevertheless, his comment lends credence to the view that even before the death of Ferdinand, the Crown was in danger of letting its immediate wealth and potential commercial gains from the New World slip through its fingers.

References

1   Helen Nader, *The Mendoza Family in the Spanish Renaissance, 1350-1550* (Rutgers University Press, New Brunswick, 1979), p. 115.
2   Stephen Haliczer, *The Comuneros of Castile: The Forging of a Revolution, 1475-1521* (University of Wisconsin Press, Madison, 1981), p. 61.
3   Jaime Vicens Vives, 'The Economy of Ferdinand and Isabella's Reign' in J. L. Highfield (ed), *Spain in the Fifteenth Century, 1369-1516* (Macmillan, 1972), p. 273.
4   Henry Kamen, *Spain, 1469-1714: A Society in Conflict* (Longman, Essex, 1991), p. 52.
5   Huguette and Pierre Chaunu, *Séville et l'Atlantique, 1504-1650* vol. ii (SEVPEN, Paris, 1955), pp. 7-83.
6   Angus Mackay, *Money, Prices and Politics in Fifteenth-Century Castile* (Royal Historical Society, 1981), p. 22.
7   Alonso de Herrera, *Agricultura General* (1513).
8   Figures are based on Earl J. Hamilton, *American Treasure and the Price Revolution in Spain, 1501-1650* (Cambridge, Mass., 1934), p. 34.
9   Pulgar, *Crónica* vol. v (Madrid, 1943), p. 337.
10 Richard Bonney, *The European Dynastic States, 1494-1660* (Oxford University Press, 1991), p. 459.

Essay questions on this chapter appear in the study guide at the end of Chapter 5 (see pages 86-7).

Social Links	Economic Trends

Social Links	Economic Trends
Crown	Agriculture - Mesta strengthened - Limited food supplies
Nobility	Trade - *Consulados* introduced - Guilds reformed - American links established
Peasants Merchants	Commerce - Currency stabilised and standardised
Urban Groups	Industry - Quality cloth produced - Under-investment in other industries
The Poor	Transport - No improvements - Tolls impeded traffic
Some upwards social mobility but limited and localised	Mainly economic continuity but with some notable elements of change

Summary - Social and Economic Issues

CHAPTER 5

Religion in the Reigns of Isabella and Ferdinand

In Chapter 1 we saw that the religious condition of Castile and Aragon in the fifteenth century was quite unlike any other European country. For more than 250 years Christianity, Islam and Judaism had coexisted side by side in a condition known as *convivencia*. Christianity was the predominant faith but the minorities were more than tolerated and, in the case of Aragon, fully integrated into society. Nonetheless, change was in the air as fluctuating social and economic conditions caused attention to be focused on wealthy Jews and *Conversos* (Jews who had been converted to Christianity), and calls grew louder for a crusade against the Muslim kingdom of Granada and the *Mudéjars* (Muslims living under Christian rule) in Castile and Aragon. The continuing existence of these minority faiths occupied the thoughts of the Catholic Monarchs for most of their reigns. This chapter will explore the religious aims of Isabella and Ferdinand, examine their relationship with the Catholic Church, and consider how far the Spanish clergy met the needs of the people. It will investigate why and with what consequences the Inquisition was introduced into Spain, account for the subsequent expulsion of the Jews, and seek to explain why the Muslims in Aragon and Castile were treated so differently. Did the Catholic Monarchs pursue a consistent religious policy? Have historians exaggerated their achievements?

1 Christianity and the Catholic Monarchs

Isabella and Ferdinand intended changing the Spanish Church in three ways: they wanted to improve the spiritual condition of the clerical and lay subjects; to reform the standard of the monastic orders; and to secure control over all clerical appointments. Each of these aims resulted in conflict: in the first case, between clerics who wanted church reforms and local communities who resisted change; in the second, between Conventual and Observant friars; and, in the third, between the Crown and the Papacy.

a) The Condition of the Secular Clergy and Laity

The Catholic Church in Spain was often criticised by visiting scholars and theologians. In 1478 the need to have resident bishops, celibate clergy and regular visitations was called for by Carrillo, Archbishop of Toledo, but little was accomplished. Cases of absenteeism, married clergy and monks who had not taken holy orders continued to be reported throughout this period. In 1492, for instance, 14 sacristans and chaplains in Ávila were found to be married. In 1500 the Bishop of Palencia had to remind his clergy not to 'gamble or fight bulls or ring or dance in public' and, in the same year, the Queen reprimanded the Bishop of Calahorra because, in his diocese, 'the greater part of the clergy are said to be and are in concubinage publicly and if our justice intervenes to punish them they revolt'. Archbishop Cisneros (1495-1517) experienced a similar lack of chastity in his cathedral of Toledo and chose to drop his investigations when he was threatened with an armed uprising by the clergy. According to the historian José Garcia Oro, the archbishop censored subsequent findings of the 1499 and 1503 visitations rather than openly confront his cathedral clergy.

Isabella was a very pious queen and undoubtedly wanted to raise the quality of her bishops, but neither she nor her husband helped as much as they might. She expected her bishops to take an active part in the government of Castile and this necessitated frequent absences on diplomatic and state business. Each of the seven bishops appointed to Córdoba between 1476 and 1510 was a royal servant and administrator, and absenteeism seems to have been an occupational hazard. Archbishop Cisneros, confessor to the Queen and royal councillor, never personally conducted a pastoral visitation of his diocese. And what chance did Ferdinand have of eliminating corruption when he himself fathered two illegitimate children and secured for his nine-year-old natural son the archbishopric of Zaragoza!

In fact, most Spaniards neither wanted nor welcomed a reformation and instead held firm to a combination of irregular practices, popular superstitions and orthodox Christianity. In her recent study of Cuenca, Sara Nalle has shown that most people were strongly attached to their traditional beliefs and local rituals. What appealed to them were the practical and participatory aspects of Catholicism - the devotion to saints, the attendance at religious processions and pilgrimages organised by confraternities, and the celebration of fast days and masses.

Yet, in spite of rather than because of popular demand, a handful of bishops led by Mendoza, Talavera and Cisneros tried to improve the moral and spiritual condition of their flock. Mendoza, Archbishop of Toledo (1482-95), founded the College of Santa Cruz to train priests at Valladolid; and Talavera, Archbishop of Granada (1492-1507), led a saintly life, resided in his diocese, and devoted his energy to helping his clergy and poorer subjects.

Cardinal Cisneros was confessor to the Queen from 1492 and Primate of Castile from 1495. His interest in humanism and his personal asceticism suggest that he shared many of the qualities of his contemporary reformers, Erasmus of Rotterdam and Savonarola of Florence, but he lacked the trenchant wit of Erasmus and the zeal of Savonarola, and had no wish to lock horns with the established Church. Instead Cisneros concentrated much of his efforts on scholarly pursuits and is remembered for four major publications - the Toledan liturgy, a translation of the complete works of Aristotle, several devotional works, and the Polyglot Bible. The Polyglot, a translation of the Bible in Latin, Greek and Hebrew, was begun in 1502 and completed after his death by scholars from the Alcalá University. This institution had been founded by Cisneros to improve the quality of theological training, and, together with his humanist scholarship, helped lay the foundations of the Catholic Reformation in Spain in the reign of Charles V (1516-56). For the present, however, most Spaniards experienced few if any changes to their religious lives and were largely untouched by the ideas flowing from Cisneros's pen.

b) Monastic Reform

Reform of the three principal monastic orders in Spain - the Dominicans, Franciscans and Benedictines - was long overdue, but papal permission was required and was only granted to Isabella and Ferdinand at the accession of Pope Alexander VI in 1493. Benedictine nuns in Galicia had long been suspected of lax practices, but a series of visitations inspired by Isabella revealed that corruption was deeply entrenched and recommended that the best course of action was to re-house them all in a single convent. The Dominicans were reformed principally by Pascual de Ampudia, Bishop of Burgos, and Diego de Deza, Archbishop of Seville. The most important order, which lived by begging, was the Franciscans. When Cisneros became their leader in 1494, he began to remove the Conventuals, a group who had abandoned their pastoral and community work in favour of a monastic life. The Queen and the Papacy welcomed his reforms but were soon questioning the slow pace at which they were occurring. Indeed, he actually restrained the activities of Juan de Guadalupe, the most outspoken Franciscan friar of his day, who believed that all friars should be forced to join the Observants. They favoured a strict 'observance' of their monastic vows. Cisneros's work, moreover, was confined to the 80 convents in Castile. A larger number lay outside his province in Aragon and they, together with other mendicant orders in Catalonia and Valencia, resisted reforms until Ferdinand put his weight behind the Franciscan Observants in the early sixteenth century.

c) The Papacy and Clerical Appointments

The Catholic Monarchs had numerous clashes with the Papacy but none was serious enough to threaten a schism and there was no reason to suggest that this would happen as long as the Crown got what it wanted and the Papacy received Spanish support in its fight against Islam. Disagreements occurred over three related issues.

First, the Crown resented the Papacy appointing foreign clerics who then absented themselves from their livings but continued to collect a salary. Although all clerical appointments were in the gift of the Papacy, this right to control ecclesiastical patronage was initially challenged by Isabella when she appointed her own nominee to the bishopric of Cuenca in 1479. Three years later the principle was established that the Crown would nominate bishops and the Papacy merely confirm them. In 1486 Innocent VIII conceded further ground when he allowed the Catholic Monarchs control of all clerical patronage in Granada and the Canaries. When this was extended to the New World in 1508, precedents had been established which successive Spanish kings would apply to their mainland kingdoms as well.

Second, from 1488 the Crown declared that the right to appeal against any ecclesiastical judgement would be heard in Valladolid rather than in Rome. This transfer of litigation resulted in a loss of revenue for the Papacy and a reduction in its secular authority in Spain but it does not seem to have harmed Hispano-Papal relations.

Third, both the Crown and the Papacy agreed that the heretical Muslims must be stamped out but, whereas Isabella believed that a war against Granada was vital, the Papacy wanted an international crusade against the Turks. Arguments thus centred on priorities and how much papal funding should be directed exclusively to Spanish projects. Pope Sixtus IV (1471-84) was very cooperative. In 1482 he granted Isabella a *cruzada*, a tax specifically intended to fund the war against Granada. Together with the *tercia real*, a payment of one-third of Castilian tithes, traditionally remitted to the Crown, papal taxes and concessions raised more than 800 million *maravedís* by 1492. In spite of occasional altercations with Pope Innocent VIII (1484-92), when he tried to increase his share of clerical revenue and called for a war between Christendom and the Saracens, relations between Spain and the Papacy remained essentially sound. As the reigns of Ferdinand and Isabella progressed, more and more papal taxation was channelled into the Treasury. Alexander VI (1492-1503) allowed the *cruzada* to be collected even after the war against Granada had ended and Pope Julius II (1503-13) extended it indefinitely in 1508 to finance Spanish campaigns in Italy, France and the New World.

2 Judaism and the Catholic Monarchs

a) The Introduction of the Inquisition, 1478

In 1477 Isabella had declared: 'All the Jews in my realms are mine and under my care and protection.'[1] Fifteen years later, they were expelled from Castile and Aragon. Few could have foreseen such a dramatic turn of events which ended several hundred years of *convivencia*. How did this come about?

Judaism was a minority faith and, like most minorities, Jews were attacked in times of economic and social unrest. Since the pogrom of 1391, an uneasy calm had settled in towns where large Jewish communities prospered. Periodically, as in 1449 at Ávila and Toledo, anti-Semitic riots broke out as Christians voiced their resentment against rich Jewish families and their economic and political influence. Many were seen as sponges who absorbed the wealth of Castile, profited from rather than contributed to society, and whose way of life was alien to the Catholic Spaniards. Of greater concern to many Christians was the growth in *Conversos*, who were entitled to full civil liberties and equal opportunities of advancement. Stories abounded that many *Conversos* practised their Jewish faith in secret and the unstable political climate of the early 1470s generated further anti-Semitic demonstrations in Toledo, Córdoba, Seville and Ávila.

It was during Isabella's visit to Seville in 1478 that a Dominican prior, Alonso de Hojeda, warned her of the imminent threat of false converts. An enquiry conducted by the Archbishop of Seville and the Prior of Segovia confirmed Hojeda's warning and persuaded the Queen that the problem was not confined to Seville and Andalucía but was rife throughout Castile. Isabella was stunned. Some of her closest friends were *Conversos*, like her secretary, Pulgar, and most noble houses in Aragon had Jewish blood. She decided to ask the Pope to let her establish a Castilian Inquisition and, following his consent in 1478, it was introduced in 1480 under the supervision of two Dominican inquisitors.

Historians have offered several reasons for the ensuing persecution of the *Conversos*. Contemporaries like Bernáldez and Pulgar believed that there were many secret judaizers, and there is much evidence in the archives of the Holy Office to support their beliefs. Certainly feeling was widespread - and corroborated by Pulgar - that many Jews were ready to inform against *Conversos* whom they saw as traitors to their faith. An alternative view, however, is that the Inquisition wished to remove both Jews and *Conversos* from Castile and, as it had no jurisdiction over the Jews, it set out to prove that *Conversos* were in regular contact with them. The truth probably lies somewhere in between: some *Conversos* were practising Jews and others were practising Christians.

Not everyone in Castile welcomed the Inquisition. Cardinal Mendoza and Bishop Talavera urged the Queen not to introduce it: there was no precedent and, although it had no official jurisdiction over bishops, they feared that it would threaten their episcopal authority. In Talavera's opinion, 'heresies need to be corrected not only with punishments and lashes, but even more with Catholic reasoning'.[2] The chronicler Pulgar suggested that a policy of preaching and persuasion should first be tried, and Seville and Toledo petitioned against its establishment. Nonetheless, Isabella would not change her mind and in the course of the 1480s tribunals were operating in nine Castilian towns.

Ferdinand introduced the Inquisition into Aragon in 1481 but his motives for doing so were quite different from Isabella's. There was no serious *Converso* or Jewish problem in Aragon and he saw the chance of establishing a tribunal under his own control, independent of Castile and the Papacy. When Sixtus IV in 1482 tried to bring it under episcopal control, Ferdinand, suspecting that the Pope was under pressure to revoke his earlier bull, wrote a stinging reply. He declared: 'If by chance concessions have been made through the persistent and cunning persuasion of the said *Conversos*, I intend never to let them take effect. Take care therefore not to let the matter go further, and to revoke any concessions and entrust us with the care of this question.'[3] The Pope submitted and agreed to the appointment of Tomás de Torquemada, Prior of Segovia, as the Inquisitor General of Aragon, Valencia and Catalonia in 1483. This Dominican monk was already well known to Isabella. As her chief inquisitor in Castile and later the first President of the Suprema in control of the Spanish Inquisition, Torquemada was one of her most loyal and devoted servants.

Opposition in Aragon to the Inquisition was even more vociferous than in Castile. A tribunal had existed in the fourteenth century but its revival was opposed not because of its novelty or intent but because its officials were Castilian. In 1484 the Catalan Corts informed Ferdinand that the inquisitors were 'against the liberties, constitutions and agreements solemnly sworn by Your Majesty', and the Comunidad of Teruel offered a similar explanation as to why they had prevented inquisitors from investigating *Conversos*. The King was unmoved by their arguments. When the Valencian and Aragonese Cortes suggested that there was no need for an Inquisition, he issued a circular letter claiming that he had 'no intention of infringing the *fueros* but rather of enforcing their observance ... If there are so few heretics as is now asserted, there should not be such dread of the Inquisition'.[4] Any doubts that the Aragonese may have had about its justification were dispelled in 1485 when an inquisitor was murdered by *Conversos* in Zaragoza cathedral. A wave of arrests followed, and popular opinion began to turn in favour of the Inquisition. Even Catalonia yielded, and Barcelona held its first tribunal in 1487.

b) The Inquisition at Work in the 1480s

In 1480 the Cortes of Toledo endorsed the Catholic Monarchs' intention to quicken the pace against the *Conversos*. Existing decrees, which ordered all Jews to be confined to ghettos (or *aljamas*) in their towns and to wear distinctive yellow badges, were enforced. Although in practice this policy of segregation was not uniformly applied, towns such as Medina del Campo, Ávila and Seville enforced it. If the aim was to isolate Jewish families and so prevent contact with the *Conversos*, its effect was to harden popular attitudes against the Jews. Some local authorities passed by-laws against them. In Segovia, where there were some 50 Jewish families, they were told not to buy food during working hours nor fish on Fridays. At Medina del Campo, Jews could not sell bread or firewood, and in Bilbao, any Jewish merchant who slept there overnight was fined 2,000 *maravedís*. Jews were subjected to heavy taxation, allegedly to pay for the Granada war, but the sums collected often amounted to 25 per cent of a town's contribution and indicate that Jewish families were the targets of definite discrimination. A handful of cities like Seville, Córdoba and Cádiz went further and expelled Jewish families.

The Spanish Inquisition in the meantime established tribunals in principal towns to investigate *Conversos*. Those suspected of reverting to Judaism were arrested, tried and, in most cases, found guilty; sentences were then passed and prisoners handed to the secular authorities to carry out the punishments. Most first offenders received lenient sentences and were 'reconciled' with the Catholic faith; few were acquitted; and those found guilty a second time were given sentences of imprisonment or death. The first to die at an *auto de fe,* a public ceremony where the accused was committed to death by burning, were six *Conversos* from Seville in 1481. A similar fate befell *Conversos* in Ávila, Toledo, Córdoba and Zaragoza in the 1480s. Although the exact number of victims may never be known, this decade was a time of great persecution. Thirty people were burnt in a single day at Ciudad Real in 1484 and the chronicler Bernáldez believed over 700 were burnt and more than 5,000 punished in Seville alone by 1488. To be suspected of holding heretical beliefs, whether proven or not, and to be the target of an investigation, was enough to convince many Jews and *Conversos* to emigrate. Some went to less hostile towns in Castile; most left for Portugal and Italy. Of course, the growing number of emigrants confirmed people's suspicions that the Jews and *Conversos* were in collusion and further justified the work of the Inquisition.

c) The Expulsion of the Jews, 1492

The Catholic Monarchs were preoccupied with another crusade in the 1480s against the Muslims of Granada but they monitored inquisitorial reports and listened to the recommendations of the Inquisitor General, Torquemada. The prevailing view was that the strategy of isolating Jews into *aljamas* to prevent them from persuading *Conversos* to backslide had not worked, and that a more effective policy was required. On 31 March 1492 a royal decree was published. All Jews had until 31 July to convert to Christianity or to emigrate. The decision, in Henry Kamen's opinion, was the logical conclusion to policies conducted in the 1480s, yet the timing of the announcement, coming less than three months after the fall of Granada, and the secrecy surrounding it - even Pulgar was shocked at the news - suggests that the Catholic Monarchs only decided upon this course of action in 1492. It is hard to accept Stephen

Haliczer's view that the suggestion came from influential *Conversos* who, fearful that the Inquisition would investigate their affairs, hoped the expulsion would deflect attention away from them. Arguments put forward by nineteenth-century historians that the Catholic Monarchs wished either to seize Jewish wealth or to establish absolute power can be dismissed: profits realised by the Crown were very small and the concept of absolutism was not a political objective of fifteenth-century rulers. In fact, the most likely influence upon the Catholic Monarchs was Torquemada. As Ferdinand explained in a letter to the Count of Aranda on 31 March 1492:

1 The Holy Office of the Inquisition, seeing how some Christians are endangered by contact and communication with the Jews, has provided that the Jews be expelled from all our realms and territories, and has persuaded us to give our support and
5 agreement to this, which we now do, because of our debts and obligations to the said Holy Office; and we do so despite the great harm to ourselves, seeking and preferring the salvation of souls above our own profit and that of individuals.[5]

Ferdinand's concern that the decree might have serious economic consequences was reiterated by an Aragonese inquisitor, who reported that: 'many were of the opinion that the King was making a mistake to throw out of his realms people who were so industrious and hard-working, and so outstanding both in number and esteem as well as in dedication to making money. They also said that more hope could be entertained of their conversion by leaving them in the country than by throwing them out.'[6]

Religious, not economic or political, considerations lay behind the decree. It is very likely that the government expected most Jews to announce their conversion rather than emigrate. In practice, perhaps one-half of all Jews converted, including some notable individuals such as the chief rabbi of Castile and the rabbi of Córdoba. In the absence of precise figures, historians continue to debate just how many Jews emigrated in the 1490s. Richard Bonney suggests there were 70,000 Castilians and 10,000 Aragonese, and Haim Beinart believes the total number was closer to 200,000, but Henry Kamen reminds us that many emigrants returned within a few years and became *Conversos*. Most historians do agree, however, that the government miscalculated by allowing the Jews insufficient time either to sell their properties if they wished to leave or to consider seriously the merits of conversion but sufficient time for them to defy the government and emigrate. The Crown did not make the same mistake in 1502 when it solved the Muslim question (see page 82): the Castilian *Mudéjars* were not given a viable alternative and almost all chose to be converted.

d) The Effects of the Expulsion

The total number of Jews who emigrated from Spain was small, constituting less than three per cent of the total population. Though the immediate economic impact on some localities will have been severe, it should be recalled that the *Conversos* rather than the Jews contributed more to the commercial and financial welfare of the kingdoms. Moreover, many Jewish families, estimated by one historian to be 40,000 strong, returned to Castile in the 1490s. If they could prove that they had been converted to Christianity, they were able to buy back their property for the same price they had sold it.

More serious were the social and religious consequences. In Kamen's opinion: 'The State turned its back on the plural society of the past, cut off an entire community that had been an integral part of the nation, and intensified the *converso* problem without solving it.'[7] The idea of *convivencia* was no longer tenable in Spain and its dominions and it also put the future of *Moriscos* (converted Muslims) and *Mudéjars* in doubt. Persecution is easy to start, but far less easy to stop. After all, if the *Conversos* were deemed to be impure and suspected of hypocrisy, so might the converted Muslims and their *Mudéjar* compatriots. The Inquisition had been accepted in Castile and, to a lesser extent, in Aragon because the Catholic Monarchs had claimed that the Catholic Church in Spain was in danger. Against a background of crusading fervour - the first decade of the Inquisition's existence had coincided with the Granada war - the secret procedures, arrests without trial, occasional use of torture and numerous deaths, became more acceptable. But the air of suspicion which surrounded its deliberations and the dubious morality of persecuting thousands of fellow subjects raised questions in the early sixteenth century about its continuation.

Complaints against the Inquisition and its officials seemed justified. Some inquisitors were brutal and corrupt and deserved condemnation. Inquisitor Bravo in Llerena, for instance, arrested as many wealthy citizens as he could find and pocketed the fines, and in Córdoba, inquisitor Lucero over a nine-year period detained 400 people without trial, burnt 134 in a six-month spell between 1504 and 1505, and even arrested the 80-year-old Talavera and his family and friends. The victims of these and other tribunals were nearly all *Conversos*, and the incidence of death was generally high. At Toledo, 250 had been burnt at the stake between 1485 and 1501, at Zaragoza 124 had died by 1502, and 99 per cent of all cases heard at the Barcelona tribunal between 1488 and 1505 concerned *Conversos*.

The expulsion of the Jews was applied to every Spanish territory except Naples which, upon annexation by Aragon in 1504, successfully resisted its introduction. Moreover, it also refused to have an Inquisition and Ferdinand, aware of the hostility that the Holy Office had generated in Sicily, did not force the issue. If the experiences of Castile and Aragon were anything to go by, the creation of the Inquisition was a mixed blessing. 'Many innocent and guiltless have suffered death, harm, oppression, injury and infamy', declared Charles V's first Cortes in 1518. 'Many of our vassals have absented themselves from these realms; and (as events have shown) in general these our realms have received and receive great ill and harm.'[8] Against this background of bloody persecution, however, should be set the claims of modern historians like Henry Kamen and Jaime Contreras. They have challenged the accuracy of the number of victims, especially those who were allegedly tortured, and have shown that the incidence of torture was often exaggerated by opponents of the Inquisition. For the moment, it would seem sensible to return an open verdict until further research has been completed.

3 Islam and the Catholic Monarchs

a) The Condition of the Spanish Muslims in 1480

It is tempting to regard the Muslims of Granada, the *Moriscos* of Castile and the *Mudéjars* of Aragon as of a piece in that they were Islamic, a minority faith, and an alien ethnic group, but this notion would be very misleading. The number of *Moriscos* in Castile in 1480 was very small and, unlike the *Conversos*, posed no serious threat to the economic and social pre-eminence enjoyed by Christians in the kingdom. The *Mudéjars* in the Crown of Aragon, on the other hand, were very numerous, totalling 30 per cent of Valencia's population, 20 per cent of Aragon's, and two per cent of Catalonia's. Nonetheless, in spite of these numbers, they were never considered a danger to Ferdinand's kingdoms. On the contrary, the King had every intention of letting them stay if they wished and knew that he could count on the support of his nobility. The existence of the Nasrid kingdom of Granada, however, was another matter as far as Isabella was concerned. Comprising some 500,000 Muslims, it was the final bastion of Islam in Iberia. Whereas Aragon had completed its reconquest in the thirteenth century, Castile's moving frontier had ceased to move. Once Isabella had secured her position on the throne, she decided to seize Granada from the Muslims once and for all.

b) The Granada War, 1482-92

Historians have long acknowledged the Queen's religious zeal. Leading by example, she inspired her subjects to improve their spiritual lives and urged them to join in her crusade against the Moors. But of equal importance at this early stage in his reign was the support given to her by Ferdinand. In 1481 he declared that he wished 'to conquer that kingdom of Granada and expel from all Spain the enemies of the Catholic faith and dedicate Spain to the service of God'. Although his sentiments may well have been sincere, both he and Isabella were keen to endear themselves to the Castilian nobility and to the Papacy. Political statements of this kind were, of course, bound to be well received. What the King did not know was that a Muslim raid on the Andalucían town of Zahara would follow in December, that it would precipitate a retaliatory strike by Christian troops against the town of Alhama, and so spark off a general war in 1482.

Castilians were confident that they would gain an easy victory. The Nasrid ruling family was riddled with factions, as became self-evident when the Emir was overthrown by his half-brother; and a nephew, Prince Boabdil, reached a deal with Ferdinand in 1483. In addition, the Muslims received no military support from their co-religionists in Aragon, north Africa or Egypt. Thus, with Ferdinand at the head of a large army, equipped with superior artillery, and with Isabella at his side in prayer, success seemed assured. Yet the Muslims proved durable fighters. By skilfully avoiding set battles and turning their towns into fortified strongholds, they forced the Christians to fight a series of long sieges which quickly exhausted both Andalucían men and money.

In 1485 the Catholic Monarchs made a dramatic appeal for more troops and supplies. Volunteers arrived in Granada from all over Castile: the Santa Hermandad, which had provided 8,000 infantry in 1483, increased its contribution by 25 per cent, and the Master of Santiago supplied 1,760 cavalry. Although foreign mercenaries also joined the crusade, what caught the attention of one contemporary was the manner in which the whole of Castile contributed to the war effort. 'Who would have thought', commented Peter Martyr, 'that the Galician, the proud Asturian and the rude inhabitant of the Pyrenees, would be mixing freely with Toledans, people of La Mancha, and Andalucíans, living together in harmony and obedience, like members of one family, speaking the same language and subject to one common discipline.' He might have added that Aragonese soldiers were also present, for it was a truly national campaign, and one led by the Catholic Monarchs. 'The King overcomes mortals, the Queen immortals' eulogised Pulgar and, as surely as Ferdinand lay siege to Moorish towns, so Isabella prayed with her troops outside Málaga in 1487 and Baza in 1489. According to legend, she even sold some of her crown jewels to help pay for the army.

In truth, the most serious problem facing the Catholic Monarchs was raising enough money to pay for supplies and troops. They negotiated loans from Castilian nobles, sold *juros* and imposed heavy taxation on their towns, the Jews and the Hermandad, but they could not have survived without massive contributions from the Church. In 1479 the Papacy had granted indulgences (money paid to the Church to reduce the length of time a soul spends in purgatory) for a crusade and three years later a *cruzada* (a 10 per cent tax on Spanish benefices and one-third of revenues from tithes). The *cruzada* had to be renewed each year and in 1484, the Crown requested that all of the tithes should be devoted to the war. In a letter dated 1485, the Catholic Monarchs claimed:

1 We neither are nor have been persuaded to undertake this war by
  desire to acquire greater rents nor the wish to lay up treasure; for
  had we wanted to increase our lordships and augment our income
  with far less peril, travail and expense, we should have been able to
5 do so. But the desire which we have to serve God and our zeal for
  the holy Catholic faith has induced us to set aside our own interests
  and ignore the continual hardships and dangers to which this cause
  commits us; and thus can we hope both that the holy Catholic faith
  may be spread and Christendom quit of so unremitting a menace
10 as abides here at our gates, until these infidels of the kingdom of
  Granada are uprooted and expelled from Spain.[9]

In fact, the Crown's motives were not so altruistic. They were as much concerned with capturing trade and land from the Muslims, with achieving national security for Castile and Aragon, and with establishing political unity in the peninsula, as they were with serving the Catholic Church. Nevertheless, Innocent VIII duly obliged and renewed the *cruzada* for the rest of the war.

As long as the Catholic Monarchs stuck to their task, they were never going to lose the war. Ronda had fallen in 1485, Málaga in 1487, and Almeria in 1489, but victory was delayed until the city of Granada surrendered in January 1492. Like imperial legionaries claiming their spoils of victory, the Catholic Monarchs accompanied by Cisneros, their servants and troops, entered the city in triumph. It was one of the highlights of their reigns, and a moment celebrated by later artists (see the illustration on page 81).

In the course of the war 100,000 Muslims had died or been enslaved and of the remaining 400,000 who surrendered, half chose to emigrate to north Africa. Those who stayed under Castilian rule were allowed to keep their own customs, laws and property, as well as their Islamic faith. The settlement was very generous and belies suggestions that the Queen was intent on imposing religious uniformity throughout her country. Perhaps she was mindful of the large number of *Mudéjars* in Granada and was reluctant to adopt a policy of forcible conversion, but it is more likely that at that time she saw the Jews as an altogether more pressing problem.

c) *Convivencia* or Persecution: Granada, 1492-1502

The decade following the conquest of Granada was for the most part a period of peaceful recovery in the traditional spirit of *convivencia*. Secular control of Granada was given to Lopez de Mendoza, the fair-minded and respected Count of Tendilla, who proved himself to be a most effective governor. The emigration of so many Muslims left large tracts of land at the disposal of the Crown. It kept most of it, but rewarded a small number of Castilian nobles with towns and estates and induced some 40,000 Andalucían peasants to settle in the more depopulated areas. The spiritual welfare of the *Mudéjars* was put in the hands of Talavera, the new Archbishop of Granada. His strategy was conciliation, believing that 'what is done for love and charity is enduring'. Matins were said in Castilian and Arabic as well as in Latin, Muslim music replaced church organs and Muslims received Christian teaching and were encouraged to abandon some of their traditional customs. Above all, Talavera convinced Isabella that the Inquisition should be kept out of the province.

Boabdil surrenders the keys of Granada to the Catholic Kings

This policy of gradual adoption and assimilation of Christian beliefs was, however, too slow for Cisneros. His intemperance is all the more surprising as he had earlier been criticised by the Queen for not tackling monastic reform more urgently. Nonetheless, in 1499 he began to enforce conversions upon *Mudéjar* communities and persuaded Isabella to introduce the Inquisition. Following a revolt in the Alpujarras mountains in January 1500, he claimed that the Crown need no longer keep to the terms of the 1492 settlement and that the *Mudéjars* 'should convert and be slaves. Because, as slaves, they will be better Christians, and the land will be made safe forever, for they are near the coast ... and are numerous'. There is no doubt that regular contact was made with the north African Moors and that, in the eyes of many Christians, the Granadan *Mudéjars* presented a security risk to Castile. Cisneros's arguments, nevertheless, have a hollow ring and suggest that he was seeking to please his patron. The King was not surprised. He knew the bishop well and considered him an intolerant man. 'As to the Archbishop of Toledo', Ferdinand declared, 'who never saw Moors, or knew them, I do not marvel.'

This more assertive strategy did, however, appeal to the Queen. Between 1500 and 1501 many *Mudéjars* were forced into conversion or emigration and a year later she extended the policy to her entire kingdom. Isabella explained her decision:

1 Considering ... that since the major cause of the subversion of many Christians that has been seen in these our kingdoms was their participation and communication with the Jews, that since there is much danger in the communication of the said Moors of
5 our kingdom with the newly converted and they [the Moors] will be a cause that the said newly converted may be drawn and induced to leave our faith and to return to their original errors ... as already by experience has been seen in some in this kingdom and outside of it, if the principal cause is removed, that is, to expel the
10 said Moors from these our kingdoms and lordships, and because it is better to prevent with the remedy than to wait to punish the errors after they are made and committed ... it is right that they be expelled.[10]

In the Queen's view then, the *Mudéjars* were the source of recent trouble and would remain so as long as they were in contact with the Moors. She had seen the effect that the Jews had had on her *Conversos*, and had no intention of making the same mistake with her *Moriscos*. Thus, from 1502, conversion or emigration was the choice facing the Castilian *Mudéjars*. The vast majority chose conversion and became *Moriscos*. *Convivencia* came to an end and the Inquisition had a new quarry to pursue.

d) The *Mudéjars* in the Crown of Aragon

Ferdinand's attitude towards the *Mudéjars* in his kingdoms was quite different from Isabella's. In his view they had for centuries played a significant part in the country's economy. As hardworking labourers and tenants, they were much valued by the nobility, and their cultural pursuits were widely respected by many Christians. The King recognised that they had remained loyal and peaceful during the Granada war and even invited a small number to move to Valencia in the 1490s. He was also more aware than Isabella of the inherent dangers of forced conversions, particularly in a kingdom like Valencia where the Muslims numbered one-third of the population. In 1500 amid rumours that he was about to take a tougher line, he declared: 'Our holy Catholic faith in the conversion of the infidels admits neither violence nor force but [only] full freedom and devotion.'[11] Ferdinand was true to his word and never converted or expelled the *Mudéjars*.

Religious tension, however, did surface in Valencia in the later years of his reign. Feelings of distrust and anxiety may have been deepened by Christians who were encouraged by Cisneros's work in Castile and Granada. A particular source of friction was the large number of mosques and the custom of calling Muslims to prayer five times a day. The presence of the Inquisition undoubtedly aggravated relations. In 1506, for example, it threatened to excommunicate and fine any official who allowed Muslims to make the call to prayer by sounding a horn, but Ferdinand and the Valencian Church overruled it and the custom continued. The King also took preventive measures to reduce the likelihood of social unrest: he ordered *Mudéjars* to live in *aljamas,* avoid sexual relations with Christians, and wear distinctive blue clothing, but attempts at segregation failed. Contact with Muslims outside the kingdoms was also restricted by preventing *Mudéjars* from entering Castile, and by limiting the number of Aragonese *Mudéjars* wishing to emigrate.

There was no violence against the *Mudéjars* in Ferdinand's reign nor were there any Muslim rebellions. The Aragonese and Valencian nobility were not inspired by the crusading spirit in Castile and the *Mudéjars* were not socially or religiously oppressed. Indeed, as long as socio-economic conditions remained stable, all groups were content with the status quo. Circumstances, however, were changing in the final years of the reign and the *Mudéjars* were to become the victims of popular hostility in the early 1520s. It was another problem which the new king, Charles V, had to face at his accession, and one which he would resolve quite differently from Ferdinand. In 1526, he expelled them from his eastern kingdoms.

4 Conclusion

The religious policy of the Catholic Monarchs was inconsistent and largely unsuccessful. Isabella 'the Catholic' was certainly more pious than Ferdinand. She worshipped daily, was accompanied by her confessor and priests wherever she went, and took an uncompromising stance towards non-Christians in her kingdom. Victory in the Granada war was the high-water mark of her reign and gave her the platform to address the question of Judaism and the *Conversos*. The thought that there were 'false converts' in Castile preyed on her conscience and, to her mind, more than justified introducing the Inquisition. By 1502 the Jews and *Mudéjars* had been expelled from Castile, and *Conversos* and, to a lesser extent, *Moriscos* were under constant investigation. Yet the pursuit of religious conformity had been accomplished at a high price. Religious and social intolerance replaced *convivencia*. Moreover, the Inquisition turned out to be more than a temporary institution and, as the self-appointed guardian of public morals, pervaded every aspect of society. By 1516 it was welcomed by few and despised by many. The more obvious need to reform the Catholic Church in Spain was tackled less enthusiastically. The primitive spiritual condition of many communities and diffident attitude to clerical corruption ensured that, in spite of a handful of reforming bishops, there was little progress overall.

Ferdinand viewed religion through a political eye-piece. He totally endorsed his wife's call for a crusade against the Muslims in Granada but he was motivated by political rather than religious reasons, and was unwilling to persecute the *Mudéjars* in his own kingdoms. Though concurring with Isabella's decision to expel the Jews, he feared that the consequences for his lands would be serious. He was less interested in encouraging reforms of the Church in Aragon and, for that matter, so was the Papacy.

Pope Alexander VI was a native of Valencia and well aware of its spiritual malaise but made no move to convene a national council to consider a reformation. Indeed, the Catholic Monarchs' relationship with the Papacy was one of the more successful features of their religious policy. They acquired control of clerical patronage, extracted papal taxes and received the endorsement of successive popes for their campaigns against the Muslims. Although the quality of popes left much to be desired, the Catholic Monarchs strengthened their secular and spiritual authority in Spain without ever seriously threatening to break with Rome.

Few states in Europe exercised as much control over their church. In France, for example, the Crown negotiated an agreement with the Papacy in 1516 by which the King elected his clergy but the Pope still confirmed the appointments and continued to collect taxation. And in England, where church-state relations were essentially very stable,

Henry VII appointed his clerics and collected papal taxes but still sought confirmation from the Papacy. Neither French nor English kings, therefore, acted as independently as the Spanish monarchs.

Some historians have claimed that Isabella and Ferdinand had one consistent and overriding aim: to achieve religious unity throughout their kingdoms. The nineteenth-century historian, Amador de los Ríos, believed that religious uniformity was the first step towards creating political unity, and that this was their ultimate goal. More recently, Joseph Pérez in his *History of Spain* (1982) has argued that the Inquisition was actually created as a secular tool to impose some unity on the diverse crowns of Castile and Aragon. The Inquisition was certainly the only institution common to all of the Spanish kingdoms and, as a political instrument, could have been conceived as a unifying agent. Yet to view its origin and work in this way is to misread its prime function. It was established to solve a religious and social problem, not to achieve religious and political unity.

Although the Castilian and Aragonese Inquisitions were united for 11 years under the command of Torquemada, in 1494 authority in Aragon passed to four bishops and, apart from the years 1504-7 when Deza was Inquisitor-General of both kingdoms, Castile and Aragon had different generals. Had Ferdinand sought to use the Inquisition as a means of achieving political unity, he would surely have continued with a single appointment. In fact, on Deza's death in 1507, Cardinal Cisneros became Inquisitor-General of Castile and Enquera commanded Aragon. As Henry Kamen has contended: 'Though the monarchs, as fervent Catholics, would have preferred the nation to be united in faith, there is in fact no evidence of a deliberate policy to impose uniformity.'[12] The Jews remained in Spain until 1492, the Castilian *Mudéjars* until 1502, and the Aragonese *Mudéjars*, *Moriscos* and *Conversos* after 1516. If the Catholic Monarchs had aimed to achieve religious uniformity, they were singularly unsuccessful.

References

1   Henry Kamen, *Inquisition and Society in Spain* (Weidenfeld and Nicholson, London, 1985), p. 12.

2   Hernando de Talavera, *Católica impugnación*, ed. F. Martin (Barcelona, 1961), p. 68.

3   H.C. Lea, *A History of the Inquisition of Spain*, vol.1 (AMS Press, New York, 1904), p. 590.

4   Lea, *Inquisition*, p. 247.

5   Pilar León Tello, *Judíos de Toledo*, vol 1 (Madrid, 1979), p. 347.

6   Jerónimo de Zurita, *Historia del rey Don Hernando el Católico*, vol 1 (Zaragoza, 1610), p. 9v.

7   Kamen, *Inquisition*, p.17.

8   Juan Antonio Llorente, *Memoria Histórica* (Madrid, 1812), pp. 119-131.

9   M.A. Ladero Quesada, *Castilla y la conquista del reino de Granada* (University of Valladolid, 1967), pp. 361-3.

10 M.A. Ladero Quesada, *Mudéjares de Castilla* (University of Valladolid, 1969), doc. 148.
11 Archivo de la Corona de Aragón, Cancillería Real, 3655:34.
12 Kamen, *Inquisition*, p. 43.

Source-based questions on *'Religion in the Reigns of Isabella and Ferdinand'*

Read the extracts from Ferdinand and Isabella on pages 76 and 82, and answer the following questions:
1 What does Ferdinand's letter to the Count of Aranda (page 76) tell you about the Spanish Inquisition? (5 marks)
2 Compare the similarities and differences of the explanations for the expulsion of the Jews (page 76) and the *Mudéjars* (page 82). (5 marks)
3 How reliable are these extracts as evidence of the Catholic Monarchs' religious policy? (7 marks)
4 How far do these documents support the view that the Catholic Monarchs were principally concerned with the 'salvation of souls' in their religious policy? (8 marks)

Answering essay questions on *'Social and Economic Issues' and 'Religion in the Reigns of Isabella and Ferdinand'*

Questions on social, economic and religious issues tend to be of two main types. A small number focus on broad social and economic topics and require an evaluation of royal policies. More common questions focus on religious issues and, in particular, on the aims and effects of Isabella's policies. Consider the following typical questions:

1 Explain the strengths and limitations of the Catholic Monarchs' economic policy.
2 To what extent was controlling the nobility the key to Isabella's successful reign?
3 How far were the reigns of Isabella and Ferdinand dominated by the policy of Reconquest?
4 Account for the motives and consequences of Isabella's and Ferdinand's religious policies.

The study guide to Chapter 3 pointed out that many questions are evaluative and require you to strike a balance between different factors. Questions 2 and 3 are of this type. Questions 1 and 4, however, are 'explanatory', asking 'Explain', or 'Account for'. Questions of this type are extremely common, and it is worth thinking about the best way to tackle them.

Think carefully about Question 4. 'Account for' requires you to supply an explanation or a series of reasons why something happened, and must not be confused with the instruction 'Give an account', which would require a narrative/description. Next you need to identify key words or phrases in the title - in this case, they are 'motives' and 'consequences'; and then you should think carefully about their meaning. Are 'motives' the same as 'aims', or does 'motives' imply a more personal element? Distinguish clearly in your own mind the differences between 'aims', 'motives' and 'reasons' as you plan your answer. 'Consequences' is the second key word. It needs to be considered in terms of short-term and long-term results, and, where appropriate, assessed rather than described. Always keep the link between 'motives' and 'consequences' clearly in mind. If your argument becomes clouded or vague, stop and re-consider whether the topic you are discussing really is a 'consequence' of one of the 'motives'. If not, think again. You might prefer to examine the motives first of all before moving to a discussion of the consequences. This is a valid approach provided you bring the two together in the conclusion. Of course, not all consequences are a direct result of a particular aim or motive, and you may need to consider religious developments in several ways. For instance, was it Isabella's intention to harm her kingdom's economy by expelling Jews and ending *convivencia*?

Few historical events can be explained by a single motive or reason, and results are also most likely to be multi-faceted. Do not be satisfied with just one explanation; it may be a 'correct' interpretation but it will not give you a comprehensive answer. Finally, when you have worked your way through the points in your plan, conclude your essay with two or three sentences. They should draw together your main explanations/ arguments and refer to the key phrases of 'motives' and 'consequences'. This will leave your teacher or examiner in no doubt about your views, which is very important. After all, these are the last words that he/she will read before deciding upon your mark.

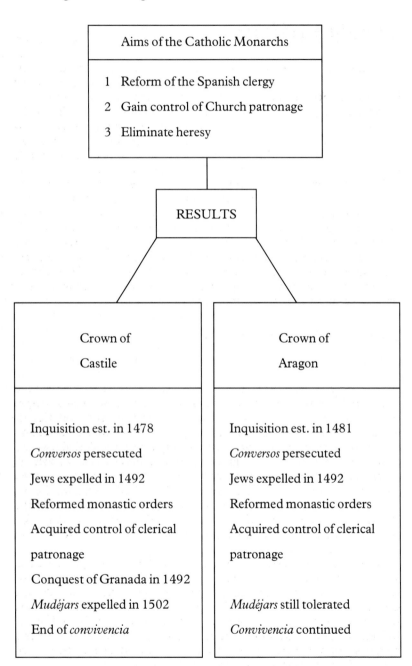

Aims of the Catholic Monarchs

1   Reform of the Spanish clergy
2   Gain control of Church patronage
3   Eliminate heresy

RESULTS

Crown of Castile	Crown of Aragon
Inquisition est. in 1478	Inquisition est. in 1481
Conversos persecuted	*Conversos* persecuted
Jews expelled in 1492	Jews expelled in 1492
Reformed monastic orders	Reformed monastic orders
Acquired control of clerical patronage	Acquired control of clerical patronage
Conquest of Granada in 1492	
Mudéjars expelled in 1502	*Mudéjars* still tolerated
End of *convivencia*	*Convivencia* continued

Summary - Religion in the Reigns of Isabella and Ferdinand

CHAPTER 6

Foreign Affairs

We have already seen that the union of Castile and Aragon raised important questions of policy-making. Decisions, whether determined by Isabella, Ferdinand, or the two acting together, had to take into account the separate customs of their different kingdoms. Thus the Castilian government and administration, its economy and society, and the attitude of Castilians towards religious groups, were quite different from those in Aragon. Their foreign relations were similarly conditioned by historical precedents and reflected diverging interests.

Foreign policy was of vital importance to a state's development in the early modern period. A ruler's reputation could stand or fall if he waged war and defended his people successfully; a country's morale could be raised if its government had a high international profile; and a state's standing was a reflection of the status of its allies, the power of its army and the acquisition of foreign lands. This chapter examines the aims, methods and policies of the Catholic Monarchs in international affairs; it considers the principal spheres of interest for Castilians and Aragonese; and it assesses Spain's standing in 1516.

1 Aims, Methods and Policies

a) Aims

Felipe Fernández-Armesto has written: 'The pursuit of a common foreign policy was based on a new community of interest, which Aragon and Castile had not previously enjoyed.'[1] Did Aragon and Castile actually have a 'common foreign policy'? Certainly once Isabella and Ferdinand were firmly in control of their kingdoms (from 1479), Aragon could take advantage of Castile's superior resources, and Castile no longer had an insecure eastern frontier. Moreover, Ferdinand assumed the dominant role in directing foreign affairs of both kingdoms: he led Castilian and Aragonese troops in battle, he negotiated marriage alliances on behalf of his wife, and he travelled to Africa and Italy. But beneath this apparent unity of purpose, there were marked differences in their foreign policies.

Isabella and her Castilian subjects desired, first, to conquer Granada and secure the north African coastline; second, to retain Portugal as an ally; and third, to develop Castile's Atlantic possessions - namely, the Canaries and, from 1492, America. That Castile should look southwards and westwards was entirely in keeping with its history. Indeed, the same spirit of territorial conquest, personal endeavour and religious zeal which imbued the war against Granada, characterised the north African and transatlantic *conquistadores*.

In contrast, Ferdinand and his Aragonese advisers were more

concerned about France, Aragon's long-standing enemy. France held Roussillon and Cerdagne, which he intended recovering; it had claims to Naples and Milan, which he intended disputing; and it had an interest in Navarre, which he intended denying. That Aragon should look northwards and eastwards reflected its need to secure the border with France and its interests in the west Mediterranean. The Balearics, Sardinia and Sicily were important trading islands en route to Naples, a kingdom ruled by Ferdinand's cousin and increasingly threatened by France and Turkey.

Both Isabella and Ferdinand, however, had one aim in common: to stem the advancing tide of Islam. Their southern and eastern coasts were prone to raids from the Barbary Corsairs; their Mediterranean possessions were open to attack from the Ottoman Turks; and their newly conquered province of Granada was always likely to receive help from the Muslims in north Africa (see the map on page 91). Writing in 1509, Ferdinand declared: 'From my youth I was always very inclined to war against infidels and it is the thing in which I receive most delight and pleasure.' A year later, he commented: 'The conquest of Jerusalem belongs to Us and We have the title of that kingdom.' Ferdinand's vehemence towards the Muslims seems at first glance to be at odds with his *Mudéjar* policy in his own kingdoms and raises questions as to the sincerity of his religious pronouncements. It should be noted, however, that Ferdinand saw nothing paradoxical about pursuing a pro-Muslim domestic policy and an anti-Muslim foreign policy. What mattered to him was the welfare of his country.

We should not be surprised therefore by Ferdinand's contrasting domestic and foreign policies. But was he really interested in leading a Christian crusade to recover Jerusalem? Did he visualise himself as the champion of Christendom or was he seeking to maintain a high international profile and, with it, the support of the Papacy? Pedro de Quintana, secretary of state, looking back on Ferdinand's life, wrote in 1516: 'The principal end and desire held by His Majesty was general peace among Christians and war against the infidel ... and he desired both these holy purposes like the salvation of his soul.' His contemporary, Niccolò Machiavelli, was of a different opinion. In his view, Ferdinand 'never preaches anything except peace and good faith, and he is an enemy of both one and the other'.[2] Ferdinand's real intentions have perplexed historians and led Garrett Mattingly to ask, rhetorically: 'Do we know how much his pious phrases were meant to deceive others, and how much to appease the uneasiness of his spirit?'[3]

b) Methods

The Catholic Monarchs conducted their foreign policy along traditional lines. First they decided in council upon a particular objective, then they constructed one or more alliances to secure their position, before finally

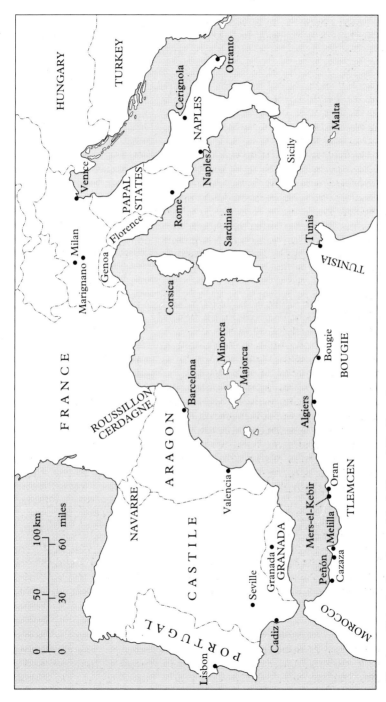

Foreign affairs in the reigns of Isabella and Ferdinand

employing whatever measures were needed to achieve their goal. Ferdinand was recognised as an expert negotiator, who made the most of limited resources. He concluded marriage alliances to strengthen Castile and Aragon's political position; he joined Holy Leagues to safeguard his Italian interests, and he made treaties with any enemy of France to accomplish his objectives. He was not averse to exploiting his allies. England was outmanoeuvred on two occasions in 1492 and in 1514, and left to wage war alone against France; Venice found itself both an ally (1495) and an enemy (1508) of Spain; and, under pretence of fighting defensively to expel an aggressor, Ferdinand emerged on numerous occasions with more territorial gains than anyone else. Well might Machiavelli claim that 'if he had ever honoured either of them [peace and good faith], he would have lost either his standing or his state many times over'.[4]

Machiavelli had been in the Florentine diplomatic service and had seen at first hand the results of Ferdinand's political dexterity. In the 1470s, several rulers had agents in foreign countries gathering information and representing their interests. Ferdinand sent ambassadors to Germany, Italy, England and the Netherlands, and in the 1490s appointed them permanently to the courts in Venice, Brussels, London and Rome. Most were legally or clerically trained Castilians, like Rodrigo González de Puebla and Juan de Sepúlveda, ambassadors in England; a few were Aragonese, and none was Italian. The efficiency of this system of gathering information and forwarding it to the royal council in Spain, however, is questionable. As there was no fixed capital, reports inevitably went astray or were lost, and royal instructions could result in contradictory orders. Nonetheless, the idea of collecting intelligence from royal courts and of having resident ambassadors in so many European countries gave Ferdinand an advantage over his rivals in international diplomacy.

In theory, peace was always preferable to war but, if necessary, Ferdinand was prepared to fight and, in the 1490s, the Spanish army came of age. Techniques in the use of artillery had been learned in the Granada war and were applied to good effect in the Italian campaigns by Gonzalo Fernández de Córdoba. This Castilian general inherited a small permanent cavalry but trained and disciplined a larger number of lightly-armoured pikemen together with a small force of arquebusiers and artillerymen, and turned them into a formidable fighting unit that was more than a match for other armies. How best to deploy the artillery was the key to military success. Córdoba, known as the 'Gran Captain' in Italy, showed that, once his cannon had breached the enemy's lines of defence, a combined attack by crossbowmen and pikemen proved invincible. The Spanish army was not always the largest force in the field but it was fast becoming the most feared.

c) Continuity or Change?

In analysing their international relations, the reigns of Isabella and Ferdinand can be usefully divided into three periods: 1479-92, 1492-1504, and 1504-16. At first, attention was given almost exclusively to waging the Granada war (see pages 78-80). Only limited resources were available to help defend Naples from the Turks and Brittany from the French, but the settlement of the Canaries, which cost little in terms of money and men, advanced apace. From 1492 to 1504, Castile and Aragon made spectacular gains. Victory over Granada raised the idea of further expansion into the heart of Africa, and the discovery of America opened up new horizons beyond the Canaries. Both ideas appealed to Castilians. Aragon, on the other hand, gained the fruits of Ferdinand's diplomatic labours, by recovering its lost Pyrenean counties and snatching Naples from the jaws of France.

The death of Isabella in 1504 changed the political climate in Spain. Ferdinand's position was less secure and Castilians glanced uneasily at his apparent preference for Aragonese projects. Cardinal Cisneros, a key member of Castile's council of state, favoured a crusade in north Africa and, for the first time, the King gave the proposal his full support. Between 1505 and 1510, several Moorish towns were captured but Ferdinand's main concern remained combatting French claims to Navarre and Milan. From 1512 to 1515, he successfully annexed Navarre and frustrated Louis XII's attempts to seize Milan, but the accession of Francis I brought fresh life to French ambitions and defeat for Ferdinand's allies at Marignano in 1515. At his death, Ferdinand left Spain with additional territories and considerable prestige, but France was in possession of Milan.

2 Castilian Interests in the West and South

a) Portugal

We saw in Chapter 2 that Alfonso V, King of Portugal, had been unsuccessful in his attempts to dethrone Isabella in the War of Succession and had made peace with her at Alcaçovas in 1479. This treaty, which laid the foundations for a long period of peace between Spain and Portugal, was further strengthened by marriage agreements between the two countries. In 1490 Isabella, the eldest daughter of the Catholic Monarchs, married Prince Alfonso, and, following his death in 1491, she married his cousin, King Manoel of Portugal, in 1497. Manoel may have aimed to unify the Iberian peninsula under his rule because, when his wife and son died, he married María, the second daughter of Isabella and Ferdinand, in 1500. In fact, in spite of Manoel's persistence, nothing came of such designs, possibly because neither Castile nor Aragon welcomed the idea. Nonetheless, the blood ties also gave the Trastámaras a claim to the Portuguese throne, one which Philip II was to assert in 1580.

b) The Canaries

At Alcaçovas Portugal had conceded to Castile all claims to the Canaries. The islands of Grand Canary, Palma and Tenerife were conquered and colonized between 1482 and 1493, and subsequently provided very important staging posts for Castilian voyages across the Atlantic. In administering the Canaries, several principles were established based on the experiences of the *Reconquista* which were to provide a blue-print for the settlement of America. Expeditions, for instance, were state and privately financed; and the Crown reserved all rights for itself and rewarded military leaders with titles, lands and goods.

One problem, however, had not been encountered before. In their desire to develop the islands' economy, the monarchs sent out water, mining and mill engineers and transported African negro slaves to supplement Canarian labour. The condition of both the Canarians and the Africans raised two important moral issues. First, were these culturally primitive and naked savages capable of reasoning, under-standing, and, by inference, self-government? A contemporary friar argued that, 'it is the law of nations that men who live and are ruled by law shall be lords of those who have no law; wherefore without sin they can take them as slaves because they are by nature the slaves of the wise who are ruled by law'. This piece of patronising logic suited the Castilian emigrants who, in a typically human way, regarded themselves as civilised and the natives as barbarians. But Isabella took a different view. She conceded that the natives might be barbarians but, in her opinion, they were entitled to their liberty. In 1477 she had ruled that they should not be enslaved, and she never deviated from this view. The Portuguese, in contrast, treated the Africans under their control as slaves - they bought and sold them like merchandise at the market in Lisbon. Portugal, of course, was more interested in developing its trade than in establishing overseas colonies and so did not face the same moral dilemma as Castile.

Second, were the natives heathens or simply ignorant of Christianity? If the former, they could be killed for their idolatry; if the latter, every attempt should be made to convert them to the Christian faith. The Queen believed that conversion was preferable to persecution but if there was any doubt as to the beliefs of the savages, then acts of aggression by the Spaniards were justified. As we shall see, these issues were magnified and highlighted by the European settlement of America.

c) America

It was immensely fortuitous for the Catholic Monarchs that Christopher Columbus should have landed in the West Indies in 1492. Isabella and Ferdinand had been preoccupied in the 1480s with their war against Granada, and, having no resources to spare, had turned down his request for patronage in 1486. Fortunately, he was also rejected by Portugal, England and France, before gaining the financial backing of a fellow Genoese in Seville and the moral support of Isabella. David Arnold has suggested: 'As late starters and as rivals of the Portuguese, the Castilians had little to lose and perhaps much to gain by sponsoring Columbus.'[5] Certainly, rivalry with Portugal was a key factor in the 1480s: its bases in west Africa were well established and it was preparing to explore the southern hemisphere and the Indian Ocean. Freed from the Granada war and inspired by victory, Isabella gave her blessing to Columbus, hopeful that he might accomplish for Castile what the explorer Diáz had achieved for Portugal. In 1487 Diáz had explored the west coast of Africa and rounded the most southerly point, naming it the Cape of Good Hope. Although there is no evidence that the Catholic

Columbus says farewell to Isabella and Ferdinand at the port of Palos de la Frontera in Andalucía

Monarchs saw Columbus off in 1492 (contrary to the illustration on page 95), they took more than a passing interest in the outcome of his voyage.

Columbus was promised the hereditary titles of admiral, viceroy, and governor of all 'the isles and continents' which he might discover, as well as ten per cent of goods and produce from the new lands. He had been confident of discovering Cathay in the East but, in fact, landed in the Bahamas, and his successive voyages in 1493-96, 1498-1500 and 1502-4 led to the discovery of Cuba, Hispaniola, Puerto Rico and Trinidad. Unlike Portugal, with its commercial and maritime overseas interests, Castile's expansion was predominantly land-based. Columbus hoped to develop the islands' economy and requested that a small number of Castilian farmers, miners and craftsmen were needed, but Isabella favoured establishing landowning colonies, whereby Spanish settlers were given *encomiendas* (large estates), and natives and imported slaves worked the land and mines.

Many settlers were drawn to America by the prospect of wealth and adventure, and a desire to spread the Christian faith. 'We came to serve God and His Majesty ... and also to get rich', declared Bernal Díaz del Castillo. Hernando Cortés was rather more candid: 'I came here to get gold', he professed in 1504, 'not to till the soil like a peasant.' Of course, these motives were incompatible, and a conflict between personal enrichment and missionary zeal assumed an even wider perspective when the treatment of the native Indians was considered.

The Amerindians, as they were known, were expected to perform labour services for the new landowners: those already holding lands were allowed to keep them but all natives had to be converted to Christianity. In return, the owner of an *encomienda* was expected to protect, instruct and educate his workers. In practice, many treated their employees as if they were slaves. A *residencia* (enquiry) into the activities of Columbus, for example, revealed several misdemeanours which resulted in his losing the governorship of Hispaniola in 1499. He had always favoured the enslavement of Indians, an idea not shared by Isabella, although she sympathised with the difficulties he and other governors had to face. In 1503 she declared that 'because of the great liberty the Indians have, they fly from conversation and communication with the Christians, so that ... they will not work, nor is it possible to teach them and attract them to our Holy Catholic Faith ... Therefore I order you to compel and force the Indians to treat and converse with the Christians and to work.'

The line between persuasion and compulsion was very fine, and could not be monitored by the Catholic Monarchs some 3,000 miles from America. They could, however, respond to eye-witness accounts. When Dominican friars arrived in Hispaniola in the first years of the sixteenth century, eager to convert the natives to Christianity, they were appalled at the way many were treated. 'Are these Indians not men?', asked Antonio de Montesinos. 'Do they not have rational souls? Are you not obliged to love them as you love yourselves?' The same questions had been raised over the Canarians, and no satisfactory answers had been forthcoming, but pressure from evangelists like Montesinos and Las Casas persuaded Ferdinand in 1512 to pass the Laws of Burgos. These stated that natives under Spanish rule must not be ill-treated; but, as subsequent administrations discovered, practices once established were difficult to eradicate. After 1516, Hieronimites and Franciscans joined the Dominicans in calling for the abolition of slavery, but their pleas fell on deaf ears.

d) North Africa

The attraction of north Africa was self-evident to most Castilians once the Nasrid kingdom of Granada had been annexed. The lure of gold, even the mythical mines of Prester John allegedly located in west Africa, had long attracted attention. Trade in ivory, shells, fish, dyestuffs and slaves indicated that there were ample profits to be made and Castilians were always looking for new supplies of wheat and spices. It has already been suggested that rivalry with Portugal was another incentive. They may have been dynastic allies but Castilians never accepted the claim made by Portuguese kings that 'the acquisition of the kingdoms of Africa belongs to us and our royal right'. The partition of the New World by Pope Alexander VI in 1494 supported the Portuguese claim when he granted them all territories in Africa and the east. But he also confirmed Castile's right to all lands in America (except Brazil) and the west, and he said nothing about the Mediterranean coast of Africa. Moreover, who could say exactly where the line was which separated east from west? Finally, the prospect of driving the Muslims out of north Africa altogether and replacing them with Castilian colonies had many attractions. It would reduce the number of seaborne attacks by pirates on the southern and eastern coasts of Spain, it would capture Muslim trade, and it would help stop the Ottoman Turks from advancing into the western Mediterranean.

In the 1480s Turkish fleets had besieged Rhodes, captured Otranto in Naples and attacked Malta. Sicily was endangered and, although Ferdinand sent military and financial aid to Naples, he was preoccupied until 1505. A plan to attack the African coast between Melilla and Orán had been drawn up in the 1490s and was now put into operation. Mers-el-Kebir was captured in 1505, Cazaza in the following year, Peñón de Vélez in 1508 and Orán in 1509 (see map on page 91). The seizure of Bougie, Tripoli and Algiers in 1510 further secured the sea routes between Sicily, Sardinia and Tunisia, opened the way for the advancement into the interior and encouraged Cardinal Cisneros to press the King to establish a north African empire. In fact, the Cardinal had personally funded and accompanied expeditions to Mers and Orán and, perhaps, regarded himself as the executor of Isabella's dying wish to continue 'the conquest of Africa and the war for the faith against the Moors'.

But the King was more influenced by commercial and political considerations than by religious zeal or visions of imperialism, and favoured setting up trading posts protected by coastal garrisons. Moreover, he really wanted to devote most of his resources to defending his territories in Italy. Although Ferdinand's decision seemed sensible at the time, it is clear that a more imaginative and bolder stroke was needed if he was not going to overstretch his empire. In fact, by not establishing colonies along the north African coast, he allowed the Barbary Corsairs (pirates) to maraud his isolated settlements and the Spanish mainland. More seriously, he failed to eliminate the threat of collaboration between the Muslims in north Africa, the *Moriscos* in Granada and the *Mudéjars* in Aragon. And, as to his promise in 1510 that he wanted to lead a crusade against Jerusalem, it was probably empty rhetoric designed to whet the appetite of his Christian supporters. Of greater concern to Ferdinand was France; it always had been and always would be.

3 Aragonese Interests in the North and East

a) Roussillon and Cerdagne

France had occupied the Pyrenean counties of Roussillon and Cerdagne since 1462, and, as King of Aragon, Ferdinand intended recovering them at the earliest opportunity. A chance unexpectedly presented itself in 1488 when King Charles VIII of France invaded Brittany. Ferdinand negotiated a treaty with Henry VII of England at Medina del Campo in 1489, whereby each would occupy French territories and force Charles to retreat. Ferdinand was busy in Granada and needed assistance from his allies but, as John Currin has demonstrated, he was a wily negotiator. For 18 months he and Henry bargained before it was agreed that 'neither would be allowed to make truce or peace with France without the consent of the other, unless Henry had received Guyenne and Normandy, or Ferdinand and Isabella had received Roussillon and Cerdagne'.[6] The likelihood of Henry fulfilling his aims was slim and Ferdinand claimed that he was unable to contribute many troops in the defence of Brittany. Thus, while English troops tried in vain to acquire lands in France, Ferdinand occupied Cerdagne and demanded the return of Roussillon. At the Treaty of Barcelona (January 1493), Catalonia recovered the Pyrenean counties and France kept Brittany. Cerdagne is still part of Spain; and Roussillon remained Spanish until 1659.

b) Naples

Ferdinand was not surprised when he heard that Charles VIII intended laying claim to Naples on the death of King Ferrante in 1494. The house of Angevin had a legitimate claim, and Charles had been immersed in diplomatic and military preparations for some time. At Barcelona, the French king had insisted that his 'just pretensions in the realm of Naples' were written into the treaty and recognised by Ferdinand. But Ferdinand was surprised at the speed with which French troops accomplished their task. Charles and 28,000 troops had crossed the Alps in September 1494 and entered Naples four months later, pushing aside paper-strong resistance. Ferdinand now decided to oust Charles and assert his own right to the kingdom, which his grandfather had once ruled. Claiming that Naples was a fief of the Papacy, whose own lands had already been violated by the French army, Ferdinand persuaded England, Milan, Venice, the Emperor and the Pope to join him in a Holy League against France in 1495.

Ferdinand may have been sincere in his belief that the 'dignity and authority of the apostolic see' must be preserved, but he kept quiet about wishing to assert his own claim to Naples. In a letter to his ambassador in London, dated January 1496, he announced that the war 'is not for any interest of our own but to aid the Pope in order that the King of France may restore what he had taken from the Church by force'.[7] Militarily outnumbered and diplomatically outmanoeuvred, Charles left Naples and, in February 1497, signed a truce with Ferdinand. The accession of a new French king, Louis XII, led the two rulers in 1500 to agree to partition the kingdom between them: Aragon would hold the south and France the north.

In fact, Ferdinand had no intention of sharing the kingdom and knew that he could provoke a border incident when he was ready. In the interim, he had been consolidating his diplomatic position and completed dynastic alliances with two of France's enemies. First, a double marriage in 1496 between Philip of Flanders and Joanna, Ferdinand's youngest daughter, and between Margaret of Austria and John, Ferdinand's eldest son, drew the Austrian Habsburgs into Spain's political circle. Second, in 1501 Arthur Tudor married Catherine, Ferdinand's third daughter, and when the English prince unexpectedly died, papal dispensations were issued permitting Catherine to marry Prince Henry (later Henry VIII). But Ferdinand had no need to call upon his Habsburg and English allies. Indeed, when he ordered General Córdoba to attack French troops in 1503, it was better that he was not handicapped by their involvement. The general's victories at Cerignola in April and at Garigliano in December led to France acknowledging Spain's sovereignty over Naples in 1504. As Isabella lay dying, Ferdinand was anxious to free himself from this war and resisted the temptation to try to drive French troops out of Italy completely. In spite of repeated French attempts to recover the kingdom, Naples remained under Spanish rule until 1714.

c) Navarre

The kingdom of Navarre straddled the Pyrenees and had been ruled by John II, King of Aragon, until his death in 1479. It then passed to Catherine de Foix and her French husband, Jean d'Albret. Although the land was economically poor and militarily vulnerable, its people wished to retain their independence and had no desire to be united with Castile and Aragon, or ruled by France. When it became a Castilian protectorate in 1494, it was on the understanding that no attempt would be made to interfere in its customs, trade or political condition.

Navarre's days of independence, however, were numbered when in 1506 Ferdinand married Germaine de Foix, a princess from a younger branch of the family who refused to accept the d'Albret right to rule the kingdom. Queen Isabella had died in 1504 and Ferdinand, aware that Germaine's brother, Gaston, was heirless, prepared to move in on Navarre. In 1512, following the death of Gaston, Ferdinand provoked a conflict. He insisted that the d'Albrets allow Spanish troops to hold key fortresses prior to their launching an attack on France and, when they refused and allied with Louis XII instead, Ferdinand invaded the country and forced them to submit. Navarre was partitioned: France held the northern lands and Ferdinand kept the south. Although in 1515 the lands were incorporated into Castile rather than Aragon, Ferdinand wisely left its institutions as he had found them. Navarre remains part of Spain today.

d) Milan

One of the main reasons why Louis XII did not help d'Albret was that the French king was in Italy laying claim to Milan and Naples. In 1509 Ferdinand had persuaded Pope Julius II to construct a Holy League against Louis. With English, Imperial, Milanese, Swiss and Castilian troops ranged against him, the French king was clearly preoccupied. In 1512 Henry VIII had been requested by Ferdinand to create a diversionary assault on France and English troops obliged by attacking the port of Brest. As French troops went to the defence of Brittany, Ferdinand seized Navarre, and in 1513 Imperial and Spanish troops drove Louis out of Milan. Thus, by 1514, Ferdinand had persuaded his allies to fight against the French aggressor while he, claiming to be the defender of Christendom, picked off Navarre.

The death of Louis and the accession of Francis I in 1515 caught Ferdinand unawares. He was himself very unwell and had decided to withdraw from Italy, after first negotiating a truce with Louis and leaving

Henry VIII to continue his own campaigns against France if he wished. As most of the English, Imperial and Spanish troops had been demobilised by 1515, Ferdinand was in no position to stop the determined young French king from invading Milan and inflicting a decisive victory over Swiss mercenaries at Marignano in September. Milan, for the time being at least, was in French hands, and Ferdinand died knowing that, at the eleventh hour, he had been outmanoeuvred.

4 Spain's Standing in 1516

Ferdinand may be excused his rather arrogant and premature boast in 1514: 'For over 700 years the Crown of Spain has not been as great or as resplendent as it is now, both in the west and the east, and all, after God, by my work and labour.' His achievements in foreign affairs - and international relations were very much his concern - were indeed considerable. The Pyrenean counties had been recovered, Navarre annexed, Granada conquered, and the Hispanic kingdoms unified. Naples had been restored, a handful of north African towns garrisoned, and the Canaries and several West Indian islands colonised. In Europe, Africa and America, Spanish settlers, administrators and soldiers took their customs, beliefs and institutions, returning enormous wealth to the Crown and prestige to their country.

No one could say where Ferdinand's legacy in international affairs would lead Castile and Aragon after 1516, but the envy of his success and fear of what the Spanish army might achieve were already apparent. The 'Black Legend' - the notion that Spain under the myth of aspiring to unite Christendom against the infidel was really intent on establishing a tyranny over the whole of western Europe - was gathering pace in Italy. When stories of enforced slavery and brutality reached Europe from America in the second decade of the sixteenth century, they confirmed many people's views of Ferdinand's amorality and took some of the gloss off his achievements. Machiavelli, the political commentator and ever a realist, admired the King and attributed his successful foreign policy precisely to his unscrupulousness. When he wrote, 'Contemporary experience shows that princes who have achieved great things have been those who have given their word lightly, who have known how to trick men with their cunning, and who, in the end, have overcome those abiding by honest principles', he had Ferdinand in mind.[8]

In fact, Ferdinand would not have been so successful if he had simply been an unfaithful and devious politician. He was a man blessed with good judgement. He knew when to abandon diplomacy in favour of war and when best to withdraw from a conflict. He was also fortunate that Portugal channelled its resources into overseas activities outside Europe, although he secured this Portuguese détente with marriage and trade agreements. Acquiring an alliance with England was a master-stroke. Henry VII was keen to strengthen his throne against

French and Burgundian threats, and an Anglo-Castilian treaty fitted neatly into Ferdinand's plans. The French monarchs, at the same time, fell prey to their own ambitions. Their attempts to assimilate Brittany and Burgundy into the kingdom of France gave Ferdinand his chance to recover his Pyrenean provinces. And in laying claim to Naples and Milan, France presented him with the perfect opportunity to extend his Aragonese empire in Italy. In an age when no country was strong enough to force its will upon another, Ferdinand recognised the importance of combining diplomacy with aggression, of building up allies and never being isolated, and thus of outmanoeuvring his enemies with the minimum of inconvenience. That he was an opportunist goes without saying, but to suggest, as Machiavelli did, that Ferdinand owed his achievements to his unscrupulousness, is to underestimate Ferdinand's qualities as a statesman.

References
1   Felipe Fernández-Armesto, *Ferdinand and Isabella* (New York, 1975), p. 186.
2   Niccolò Machiavelli, *The Prince*, ed. G. Bull (Penguin, London, 1981), p. 101.
3   Garrett Mattingly, *Renaissance Diplomacy* (Penguin, London, 1965), p. 158.
4   Machiavelli, *The Prince*, p. 102.
5   David Arnold, *The Age of Discovery, 1400-1600* (Routledge, London, 1983), p. 33.
6   John M. Currin, 'Henry VII and the Treaty of Redon (1489): Plantagenet Ambitions and Early Tudor Foreign Policy', *History*, vol. 81 (Blackwell, Oxford, 1996), p. 353.
7   *Calendar of Letters, Despatches and State Papers Relating to the Negotiations between England and Spain, Preserved in the Archives at Simancas and Elsewhere, 1485-1509,* ed. G.A. Bergenroth (HMSO, London, 1862), i, p. 82.
8   Machiavelli, *The Prince*, p. 99.

Essay questions on this chapter appear in the study guide at the end of Chapter 7 (see page 112).

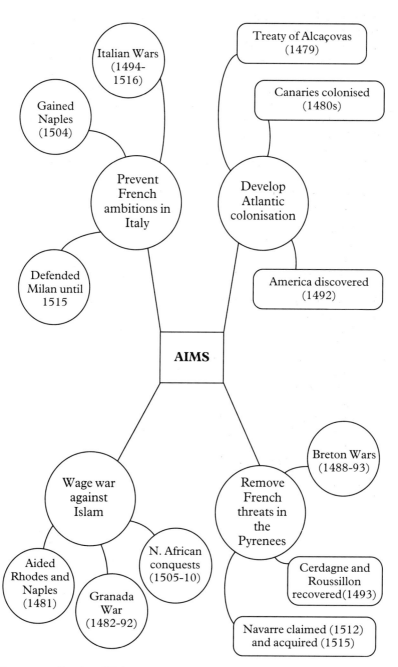

Summary - Foreign Affairs

Conclusion

This book has examined the development of the Spanish kingdoms in the reigns of Isabella and Ferdinand. Within a broad sweep of some 40 years, two separate but related themes have been traced: the role of the Catholic Monarchs in shaping the history of their peoples, and the extent to which Spain had become a united country by 1516. It is now time to form a conclusion to each of these themes.

1 The Achievement of the Catholic Monarchs

a) The Contemporary View

Contemporary Castilians had a near unanimous verdict on Queen Isabella, 'the Catholic'. She was virtuous, pious, courageous and strong-willed. She was the ideal monarch who had brought greatness to their country. She was the 'Hidden One' (*El Encubierto*), who had saved her people from anarchy and heresy, who had slayed the infidel and discovered the New World. In the words of Diego de Valera, one of Isabella's chroniclers: 'It can be said in truth that just as our Lord wished that our glorious Lady might be born in this world because from her would proceed the Universal Redeemer of the human lineage, so he determined that you, My Lady, would be born to reform and restore these kingdoms and lead them out from the tyrannical government under which they have been for so long.'[1]

For her part, Isabella encouraged her chroniclers and poets to compare her to Diana, the goddess of hunting, to call her Astraea, who had descended from heaven, and to refer to her as the 'Queen of the Amazons'. Each fifteenth-century ruler in Castile had ascended the throne amid speculation that he might be the messiah-king, the redeemer, who would save his people from damnation and lead them to the promised land. Each one had proved a failure. Isabella, it was believed, was different and, as her reign progressed, so her writers garlanded her with praise. They stressed the importance she had given to re-establishing order and discipline in her war-torn land, and the emphasis she placed on the restoration of justice. One man who remembered seeing the Queen at her Friday audiences was Fernández de Oviedo. It was, he recalled, 'a golden time indeed, and a time of justice'.

In an age when female rulers were a rarity - Isabella was the only Queen Regnant at the end of the fifteenth century - she was certainly an exceptional woman. Active in administration and government as well as in diplomatic and military affairs, she complemented the work of her husband in so many ways. An Italian visitor to Castile believed that she actually owed her authority to her partnership with Ferdinand. 'She commands in such a way that she always appears to do it in accord with her husband,' wrote Peter Martyr, 'so that the edicts and other documents are published with the signature of both'.[2] When they were apart, they kept in contact via a team of couriers who carried their letters across the peninsula. 'Love held their wills joined', declared Pulgar. He knew them well, and he was probably right.

Isabella was regarded as an extremely devout queen. She viewed religion as something real, that she had a duty to combat Satan in all his guises and to rid her kingdom of heretics. It was the Queen who had introduced the Inquisition to Castile in 1478, who had urged Ferdinand to complete the *Reconquista* (1482-92), and who had expelled the Jews (1492) and *Mudéjars* (1502) from Castile. Most of her advisers supported her and some, like Torquemada and Manrique, encouraged her righteousness. Criticism, on the other hand, was not welcomed, as Pulgar discovered. He was a *Converso* and one of the few Castilians close to the Queen who questioned the wisdom of introducing the Inquisition. Within a few weeks, he was relieved of his post of court historian. Understandably, however, such criticisms were rare. Isabella's chroniclers were expected to write favourably about herself and Castilian affairs, and Pulgar, Palencia, Valera and Bernáldez generally obliged. They portrayed the King as a second-fiddle, who responded to Isabella's lead. He was wavering and she was decisive; he was liberal and she was absolute; he was a philanderer and she was chaste.

Ferdinand, on the other hand, was regarded by Aragonese writers as a good omen. Described as the 'Bat', or hidden one, he would restore peace to his people and lead them to prosperity after years in the wilderness. And the young King did not disappoint his supporters. As a result, court propagandists like Gonzalo García de Santa María described him as a providential king, who had saved his people from the forces of darkness and had brought glory to the Trastámara dynasty. Above all, it was in the arena of international affairs that Ferdinand excelled. Machiavelli, who never met the King, nevertheless admired him enormously. 'If you study his achievements, you will find that they were all magnificent and some of them unparalleled', he declared. Machiavelli continued:

1 At the start of his reign he attacked Granada; and this campaign laid the foundation of his power. First, he embarked on it undistracted, and without fear of interference; he used it to engage the energies of the barons of Castile who, as they were giving their
5 minds to the war, had no mind for causing trouble at home. In this way, without their realizing what was happening, he increased his standing and his control over them. He was able to sustain his armies with money from the Church and the people, and, by means of that long war, to lay a good foundation for his standing
10 army, which has subsequently won him renown. In addition, in

order to be able to undertake even greater campaigns, still making use of religion, he turned his hand to a pious work of cruelty when he chased out the *Moriscos* and rid his kingdom of them: there could not have been a more pitiful or striking enterprise. Under the
15 same cloak of religion he assaulted Africa; he started his campaign in Italy; he has recently attacked France. Thus he has always planned and completed great projects, which have always kept his subjects in a state of suspense and wonder, and intent on their outcome.[3]

Machiavelli's analysis is not totally accurate - Ferdinand did not expel the *Moriscos* from his own lands, and most certainly did not deliberately attack Granada to gain control over the Castilian nobility. Nor is it entirely true to suggest that he invaded Africa and Italy 'under the cloak of religion'. What is significant about Machiavelli's assessment, however, is the importance he attached to the military achievements. 'Nothing brings a prince more prestige than great campaigns and striking demonstrations of his personal abilities', he argued. And, in this respect, Ferdinand was steeped in laurels. He had defeated the Muslims in Granada in 1492, stemmed the advancing tide of Islam in the Mediterranean and in north Africa, and, from 1495, saved the Papal States from marauding French armies in Italy. Indeed, it was on account of his services to the Papacy that Alexander VI had entitled Ferdinand and Isabella the 'Catholic Kings' in 1496. Antonio de Nebrija, court poet and historian, agreed that the monarchs' reputation rested on their foreign achievements. He wrote:

1 And now, who cannot see that, although the title of Empire is in Germany, its reality lies in the power of the Spanish monarchs who, masters of a large part of Italy and the isles of the Mediterranean Sea, carry the war to Africa and send out their fleet,
5 following the course of the stars, to the isles of the Indies and the New World, linking the Orient to the western boundary of Spain and Africa.[4]

The views of Nebrija and those of his fellow writers were understandably biased in favour of Isabella and Ferdinand, and yet their prejudice does not diminish the value of their commentaries. Contemporaries sensed that as Spain was growing in strength and power, a new age was dawning. For once, the soothsayers who had forecast this development had been proved correct.

b) Historians' Views of the Catholic Monarchs

An idealized image of the Catholic Monarchs has been accepted by most historians. 'The monarchy was falling apart at every joint; the Catholic

Sovereigns restored it on a new plan', claimed J.H. Mariéjol in 1892. Modern biographers like Tarsicio de Azcona (1964), Felipe Fernández-Armesto (1975), Joseph Pérez (1988) and Peggy Liss (1992) have been similarly fulsome in their praises. Unquestionably, the reigns of Isabella and Ferdinand saw many achievements: the unification of the Spanish kingdoms for the first time since the Roman period; the conquest of Granada and liberation of Iberia from the infidel; the discovery of America and the beginning of its colonisation; the end of civil war within Castile and Aragon, as well as between the two kingdoms; the restoration of a strong monarchy; the acquisition of lands in north Africa and Italy; and the containment of French ambitions. Any one of these accomplishments was a major triumph, and, to be successful in so many fields, may well justify the view that this was a 'golden age'.

Yet, as Isabella was all too aware, serious problems remained. In her will written shortly before her death in 1504, she expressed her regrets at the way the Amerindians had been treated; she acknowledged that land in Castile had been illegally granted to her nobility; she warned against the continuance of *juros* and called for reforms in the collection of crown revenue; and she feared that the law was still being perverted by many of her subjects. What is remarkable about her testament is that most historians have regarded it as the confession of a conscience-stricken queen rather than a just commentary on the final years of Isabella's reign. Castilian historians have therefore followed the lead of her chroniclers by praising her successes and attributing any failings to her successors, who were, of course, foreigners. In fact, Isabella's will is a very perceptive statement which identifies her anxieties and the shortcomings of her reign.

The nobility were far from subdued in 1504 and several nobles in Castile continued to act independently of the Crown. Political anarchy and domestic strife had not been totally suppressed, as was evident from the disturbances in 1506-8 and 1516-17, and from the revolt of the *Comuneros* in 1519-22. The administration of justice, finance and local government were all showing signs of corruption, and town councils expressed their growing despair at the Crown's apparent inability to reform affairs. The introduction of the Inquisition may have achieved religious uniformity, at least officially, but it also created social tensions. The Catholic Monarchs counted their crusade against the Jews and Muslims as a success but, for many, fear and uncertainty had replaced tolerance and *convivencia*. New Christians were now subject to constant harassment, and Old Christians lived under the uncertain prospect of secret investigations by the Inquisition.

Economically, the kingdoms' resources were being wasted and opportunities for investment were lost as a result of inept and muddle-headed thinking by the government. Castile's agricultural and industrial base was weak, and a policy of protectionism unwittingly restricted trade within the peninsula. The Crown's commercial prospects were further reduced when it embarked on a strategy of borrowing money from Genoese bankers, and financial matters were not assisted by Spain's growing imperial commitments. By 1516, royal expenditure was greater than its revenue. Ferdinand's international ambitions led to ill-feeling against him in Italy, to the establishment of expensive garrisons in north Africa, and to a long series of dynastic wars with France. The colonisation of the Canaries and the West Indies also brought unprecedented problems about how best to treat the natives.

Finally, the continuation of the Trastámara dynasty which, in essence, was the prime aim of the monarchs, came to an end with Isabella's death. It was obvious that when her son, John, died heirless in 1497, the succession would pass to Joanna and Philip and, after them, to their eldest son, Charles. Isabella knew that her daughter's mental condition was very unstable; what she did not know was that Philip would die in 1506 and that his death would totally unhinge his grieving widow. Ten years later Ferdinand died aware that Charles Habsburg would rule Aragon and probably Castile as well. It is ironic, therefore, that although Isabella and Ferdinand had not wanted the Habsburgs to succeed to Castile and Aragon, neither could prevent it from happening.

Historians often experience considerable difficulties in reaching a verdict. How to reconcile the achievements and failures of Isabella and Ferdinand is no exception. Was the expulsion of the Jews, for instance, a success or failure? If the conquest of Granada is regarded as an unqualified achievement for the Catholic Monarchs, does it outweigh their failure to improve their countries' economy? How do you evaluate the impact of the Inquisition? Did it fulfil its task or produce even more problems? Collectively, the triumphs of the Catholic Monarchs were far-reaching and, in many respects, unprecedented. It can also be argued that their limitations and failures were more apparent to historians writing with the benefit of hindsight than they were to most contemporaries. In reaching a conclusion, therefore, you should assess their accomplishments in the light of their aims and difficulties.

2 How Far was Spain a United Country in 1516?

a) The Contemporary View

In the opinion of most contemporaries, the marriage of Isabella and Ferdinand did more than unite two rulers - it united the medieval kingdoms of Spain. Ever since the start of the Reconquest in the eleventh century, writers had dreamed of the day when the Hispanic kingdoms would be unified under a Christian monarch. Throughout the fifteenth century, each new accession to the thrones of Aragon and Castile had been greeted with the belief that political union would soon follow, and each reign had proved disappointing. Was there a self-fulfilling prophecy about the union of Isabella and Ferdinand? Each had been second-in-line to their thrones and had not expected to succeed. Moreover, Isabella's father had opposed her marriage to Ferdinand and it had to be concluded in secret. In spite of these obstacles, the union had proved fruitful and, by adopting the symbols of F and Y, Isabella's *Flechas* (a bundle of arrows) and Ferdinand's *Yugo* (a yoke), and intertwining them figuratively on art-work and royal buildings, the monarchs seemed to be confirming the prophecy.

As the political shape of the peninsula changed, first with the incorporation of Granada into Castile, then the restoration of Cerdagne and Roussillon to Aragon, and finally with the annexation of Navarre by Castile, contemporaries realised that they were witnessing the unification of Spain. Nebrija could thus write: 'The members and pieces of Spain, which were scattered everywhere, were reduced and joined in one single body and unity of kingdom, the shape and plan of which is so ordered that many centuries, wounds, and times will be unable to break it or undo it.'[5]

Like so much of what Nebrija had to say, his comments proved far-sighted and accurate. Of course, neither Isabella nor Ferdinand was working to a pre-determined plan: the acquisition of land in the Iberian peninsula, for example, owed more to luck than design. Nevertheless, the Catholic Monarchs were persistent and ready to take opportunities whenever they arose. Whether Spain was a united country by 1516, however, is another question, and one which has interested historians for many years.

b) Historians' Views of Spanish Unity

Some historians have argued that the reigns of Isabella and Ferdinand saw the beginnings of a national identity. Ramón Menéndez Pidal, writing in 1951, believed that Isabella's insistence on putting the war against Granada before the conflict with France was 'more formative of national unity', in so far as men and money came from the whole of Iberia and bound the people together in a common cause.[6] (Of course, it was also true that Castilians regarded the war against France in Italy as an Aragon-centred policy and had little to commend it.) Furthermore John Lynch, writing in 1981, suggested that 'the makings of a nation state, united, peaceful beyond any in Europe' was the legacy of the Catholic Monarchs.[7] On the other hand, historians like Miguel Angel Ladero Quesada and Glyn Redworth have stressed the diverse characteristics of the kingdoms. They have argued that, although the idea of unity was talked about enthusiastically, it remained an idealistic concept beyond the reach of Isabella and Ferdinand. Of course, you should first decide what, exactly, characterises a united country. Is it sufficient for a state to be a geographical unit or must it be politically united as well? Indeed, can a country ever attain social and economic unity? Most historians would argue that there's no such thing as a fully united or unified state. There are only degrees.

Considerable strides towards unity had been made by the end of Ferdinand's reign. Glyn Redworth has suggested that: 'It makes better sense to think of the union as dating from the accession of Charles V in 1516.'[8] Certainly, by then one monarch ruled the kingdoms of Castile, Aragon, Valencia, Catalonia and Navarre; the army comprised troops drawn from all over Spain and its dominions; and all kingdoms shared a common unit of accounting money (the *maravedí*) and a common coin (the gold ducat). Only one faith existed in Castile (at least in theory), and there were calls to end *convivencia* in the Crown of Aragon as well. Moreover, inquisitions existed in every Hispanic kingdom and all were subject to the Castilian Suprema. Royal administration was conciliar and increasingly centred upon Castile. As yet, there was no permanent royal court but Valladolid was where Ferdinand spent most of his final years, and it was beginning to assume the role of an administrative capital.

In contrast, there is ample evidence that Spain was essentially a divided and divisive country. The political institutions of councils, Cortes and regional assemblies reflected the individuality of the different kingdoms. Each kingdom continued to cherish its autonomy and defended its constitutional liberties; and the representative estates in the Crown of Aragon were particularly sensitive to outside interference. Crown officials, especially the *corregidores*, had only a minimal impact as insufficient numbers operated in Castile, while there were none at all in Aragon. The Hermandad had the potential to expand into a supranational institution but was widely resented. Indeed, although it functioned throughout Castile for 15 years, it was terminated in 1498 and had but a brief existence in Aragon. Economic barriers remained within and between the kingdoms and the perpetuation of their different currencies was a powerful reminder of their separate economies. Even the Inquisition, the only institution common to all of the Hispanic kingdoms, caused deep resentment in both Castile and Aragon. Nor should it be forgotten that it was conceived and used as an instrument of religious uniformity not political unity. The monarchs had no plans to use the Suprema as a political weapon, and, as their differing attitudes towards the *Mudéjars* confirms, Castilian and Aragonese institutions had little in common either in politics or in religion.

There is little evidence that either of the Catholic Monarchs aspired to achieve a unitary state. They never used the title 'Kings of Spain', and they recognised the limits of their power outside their own kingdom. As surely as Isabella could not inherit Aragon, so she prevented Ferdinand from inheriting Castile by bequeathing her kingdom to Joanna and her son, Charles. Ferdinand also contemplated keeping the Hispanic kingdoms under different rulers. In his will of 1512, he granted his Aragonese empire to Prince Ferdinand, the younger brother of Charles, and only revoked his will in favour of Charles in 1515, probably on the advice of Cisneros. The acquisition and administration of Naples, Navarre and the New World also reveal the monarchs' belief in a pluralist state: Naples was incorporated into the Crown of Aragon, Navarre was annexed to Castile, and trade with the New World was granted exclusively to Castile. There was no question of integrating the resources of the five kingdoms, no desire to extend Castilian practices to Naples and Navarre, and no intention to allow the eastern kingdoms access to the markets of America.

Isabella and Ferdinand did not bequeath a united country, but just how disunited was it? How centralised were its political and administrative institutions? Was it economically and socially very diverse? Was it deeply divided religiously, ethnically and linguistically? In seeking answers to these questions, and to assess the achievements of the Catholic Monarchs, you should remember that in 1516, in spite of these divisive elements, Spain stood on the threshold of European greatness. It was a triumph of determination over adversity, a tribute to the personal rule of Isabella and Ferdinand.

References

1   Diego de Valera, *Prosistas españolas,* ed. Mario Penna, 2 vols. (Madrid, 1959), no. 17.
2   Peter Martyr, *Epistolario,* epistle 31, printed in *Documentos inéditos para la Historia de España* (Madrid, 1955).
3   N. Machiavelli, *The Prince, 1513,* ed. G. Bull (Penguin, London, 1981), pp. 119-120.
4   Cited in Ramón Menéndez Pidal, 'The Significance of the Reign of Isabella the Catholic, According to Her Contemporaries' in J.R.L. Highfield (ed), *Spain in the Fifteenth Century, 1369-1516* (Macmillan, Basingstoke, 1972), pp. 401-402.
5   Menéndez Pidal, 'The Significance of the Reign of Isabella the Catholic', p. 400.
6   Menéndez Pidal, 'The Significance of the Reign of Isabella the Catholic', p. 392.
7   John Lynch, *Spain Under the Habsburgs* (Oxford University Press, 1981), reprinted as *Spain 1516-1598: From Nation State to World Empire* (Blackwell, Oxford, 1991), p. 1.
8   Glyn Redworth, *Government and Society in Late Medieval Spain,* New Appreciations in History, 31 (Historical Association, London, 1993), p. 25.

Answering essay questions on 'Foreign Affairs' and 'Conclusion'

Questions on foreign affairs tend to fall into three main types. They can focus on an assessment of the aims, methods and achievements of the Catholic Monarchs' foreign policy, on the significance of a particular policy, or on the relative importance of foreign affairs in the broader context of their reigns. Questions that call for an overview of the whole period understandably require a balanced response, which should cover both domestic and foreign affairs. The most popular questions target particular issues, such as the unity and stability of the kingdoms, or they require an overall assessment of the Catholic Monarchs' rule. Consider the following typical questions:

1   How far did Isabella and Ferdinand achieve the aims of their foreign policy?
2   Assess the importance of foreign affairs in accounting for the successes of Isabella and Ferdinand.
3   How far and why can Spain be regarded as a more stable country in 1516 than at the accession of Isabella in 1474?
4   'Isabella and Ferdinand established a dynastic union but not a united country.' Discuss.

Questions 1 and 2 are evaluative type questions, which we examined in the study guide in Chapter 3; and Question 3, which requires an explanation as well as an assessment, was considered in Chapter 5. Question 4, however, invites a discussion. This open-ended approach to a topic can initially present a few problems since the interpretation and structure of your answer rest entirely in your hands. The key to your success lies in careful preparation, thinking and planning before you begin to write your essay.

Look at Question 4, and decide what are the most important words or phrases. In this case, they are 'dynastic union' and 'united country'. Then think carefully about their meaning. The concepts of 'union' and 'unity' need to be considered first, and, to do this effectively, it may help if you ask a number of sub-questions. For example, were the kingdoms unified administratively as well as politically? Did the monarchs' religious policies in any sense unify Spain? Did Castile and Aragon develop separate or similar economies? Was a common foreign policy pursued? Questions of this kind will help you to construct sections or paragraphs which will enable you to discuss your ideas and explanations.

Evidence of 'unity' or 'disunity' can best be obtained by reading your class notes, and by making notes from textbooks and historical articles. This is a slow but necessary process, and there are no short-cuts. All essays should be a combination of facts and arguments. Getting the right balance is not easy: there must be enough facts to 'prove' an argument but not so many that the reader is left overwhelmed and confused. As you read, you will not only gather information; you will also gain ideas, some of which may cause you to re-think your original interpretations. You should not be put off by this. Reading and re-assessment are vital parts of an historian's training. In this essay, your reading will help you to shape your ideas about 'how far' Spain was a united country by 1516. As we saw in the study guide in Chapter 3, this requires you to make a value judgement: 'to what extent' was there partial or complete unity, and, by inference, how far was there an absence of unity? Of course, the degree to which Spain became a united country has been a recurring theme of this book. You will find Chapter 7 particularly useful as it draws together several features examined in the earlier chapters, but it should be used in conjunction with Chapter 1 which considers the condition of the Hispanic kingdoms in 1469.

Successes

1 Civil wars ended
2 Crown lands recovered
3 Granada conquered
4 New World discovered
5 Increased overseas empire

Signs of Unity

1 Political union of the kingdoms
2 Suprema controlled the inquisitions
3 *Maravedí* was the unit of accounting
4 Armies recruited from all kingdoms
5 Valladolid emerged as the centre of administration

Aragon and Castile under the Catholic Monarchs

Signs of Disunity

1 Different political institutions
2 Economic barriers and no free trade
3 Regional linguistic variation
4 Different currencies in operation
5 Aragonese culture and religion still pluralistic

Failures

1 Nobility not curtailed
2 Church encouraged uniformity rather than *convivencia* in Castile
3 Corrupt and unfair financial system
4 Defective industrial and agricultural base
5 Foreign acquisitions brought as many problems as benefits

Summary - Conclusion

Chronological Table

1469 Marriage of Isabella and Ferdinand
1470 Henry IV renounces Isabella in favour of Joanna as his heir
1472 Catalonian war ends
1474 Accession of Isabella to the throne of Castile
1475-9 War of Succession in Castile
1476 Santa Hermandad set up; Battle of Toro between Castile and Portugal
1477 Seville surrenders to Isabella
1478 Inquisition introduced into Castile
1479 Accession of Ferdinand to the throne of Aragon; Treaty of Alcaçovas ends Castile's war with Portugal
1480 Cortes of Toledo hears Isabella's plans to reform her kingdom
1481 Inquisition re-established in Aragon
1482 Granada war starts
1483 Torquemada becomes first Inquisitor General of Spain
1486 Sentence of Guadalupe liberates the *remensa* peasants
1488 Brittany war begins
1489 Treaty of Medina del Campo is signed with England
1492 Granada falls and the kingdom is incorporated into Castile; Jews in Castile and Aragon are expelled; Columbus starts his transatlantic voyage
1493 Roussillon and Cerdagne recovered by the Treaty of Barcelona
1494 Alexander VI confirms the Treaty of Tordesillas which divided the New World between Castile and Portugal
1495 Princess Joanna marries Philip the Fair
1496 Ferdinand and Isabella are granted the title of 'Catholic Monarchs'
1497 Prince John dies
1498 Santa Hermandad is dissolved
1499 *Mudéjar* revolt in Granada
1500 Birth of Charles Habsburg, son of Joanna and Philip
1502 Castilian *Mudéjars* forced into Christianity or emigration
1503 Birth of Ferdinand, brother of Charles; *Casa de Contratación* set up
1504 Aragon acquires Naples from France; Death of Isabella
1505 Ferdinand marries Germaine de Foix (announced in 1506)
1506 Philip dies; civil disturbances throughout Castile
1508 Alcalá university opens; Ferdinand assumes regency of Castile
1509 Orán in north Africa is seized
1510 Bougie, Tripoli and Algiers are captured
1511 Ordinances of Seville establish regulations for industrial workers
1512 Spanish Navarre annexed by Castile
1515 Battle of Marignano secures Milan for France
1516 Death of Ferdinand

Further Reading

1 General Books on European History

D. Arnold, *The Age of Discovery, 1400-1600* (Routledge, 1983) - a useful introduction to the establishment of European overseas empires.

R. Bonney, *The European Dynastic States, 1494-1660* (Oxford University Press, 1991) - a far-reaching analytical study, which sets the reigns of the Catholic Monarchs in a wider perspective.

J. Lotherington (ed), *Years of Renewal* (Hodder and Stoughton, 1988) - a good introduction to Spanish History, suitable for the average sixth former.

2 Spain

T.N. Bisson, *The Medieval Crown of Aragon* (Oxford University Press, 1986) - the most recent work in English on Aragonese institutions, society and monarchy. It is an indispensable guide to understanding this period.

W.A. Christian, *Local Religion in Sixteenth-Century Spain* (Princeton University Press, 1981) - a highly readable survey of religious beliefs and customs.

J.H. Elliott, *Imperial Spain* (Pelican, 1963) - still regarded as a useful introduction to early modern Spanish history.

S. Haliczer, *The Comuneros of Castile: The Forging of a Revolution, 1475-1521* (University of Wisconsin Press, 1981) - a challenging and worthwhile book, which examines the underlying political and social tensions of this period.

J.R.L. Highfield (ed.), *Spain in the Fifteenth Century, 1369-1516* (Macmillan, 1972) - contains a variety of essays best suited to the specialist.

J.N. Hillgarth, *The Spanish Kingdoms, 1410-1516,* vol 2 (Clarendon Press, Oxford, 1978) - a useful source of background information.

H. Kamen, *Spain 1469-1714: A Society in Conflict* (Longman, 1991) - a very detailed narrative and analysis, particularly strong on religious themes.

A. Mackay, *Spain in the Middle Ages* (Clarendon Press, Oxford, 1977) - an excellent general history of Spain in the fifteenth century.

W.D. Phillips, *Enrique IV and the Crisis of Fifteenth-Century Castile, 1425-1480* (Medieval Academy of America, Cambridge, Mass., 1978) - the author demonstrates in this revisionist study how and why Henry's reputation was distorted by contemporary writers.

3 Isabella and Ferdinand

J.H. Edwards, *The Monarchies of Ferdinand and Isabella,* New Appreciations in History, 36 (Historical Association, London, 1996) - a highly readable introduction.

F. Fernández-Armesto, *Ferdinand and Isabella* (New York, 1975) - a general survey which uncritically describes their lives and reigns.

M.A. Ladero Quesada, *Los Reyes Católicos: La Coruña y la Unidad de España* (University of Valladolid, 1989) - the most recent assessment of the government and administration by one of Spain's leading historians.

P.K. Liss, *Isabel. The Queen* (Oxford University Press, 1992) - the latest biography which arguably offers a romanticised view of Isabella.

J. Pérez, *Isabel y Fernando. Reyes Católicos de España* (Madrid, 1988) - the most recent assessment in Spanish of the Catholic Monarchs.

4 The Spanish Government

S. Haliczer, 'The Castilian Aristocracy and the Mercedes Reform of 1478-82', *Hispanic American Historical Review,* 55 (1975) - a detailed article which examines the significance of Isabella's early fiscal reforms.

M. Lunenfeld, *Keepers of the City* (Cambridge University Press, 1987) - the *corregidores* are the subject of this study, although it offers valuable insights into other aspects of domestic affairs.

M. Lunenfeld, *The Council of the Santa Hermandad. A Study of the Pacification Forces of Ferdinand and Isabella* (University of Miami Press, 1970) - a very readable survey of fifteenth-century royal justice in Castile.

G. Redworth, *Government and Society in Late Medieval Spain,* New Appreciations in History, 31 (Historical Association, London, 1993) - a concise and thoughtful introduction to medieval Castilian government, administration and society.

5 Society and the Economy

H. and P. Chaunu, *Séville et l'Atlantique, 1504-1650,* vol. 1 (SEVPEN, Paris, 1955) - an invaluable collection of statistics relating to Spain's trade with America.

A. Mackay, *Money, Prices and Politics in Fifteenth-Century Castile* (Royal Historical Society, 1981) - a specialist work by an expert in this field.

H. Nader, *The Mendoza Family in the Spanish Renaissance, 1350-1550* (Rutgers University Press, 1979) - an interesting study of one of the most powerful families in Castile.

J. Vicens Vives, 'The Economy of Ferdinand and Isabella's Reign' in **J.L. Highfield** (ed), *Spain in the Fifteenth Century, 1369-1516* (Macmillan, 1972) - a basic but useful essay from one of Spain's best economic historians.

6 Religion

H. Kamen, *Inquisition and Society in Spain* (Weidenfeld and Nicolson, 1985) - an informed study of the origin, work and impact of the Spanish inquisition.

A. Mackay, 'Popular Movements and Pogroms in Fifteenth-Century Castile', *Past and Present,* 55 (1972) - an article which traces anti-Semitic activities.

M. Meyerson, *The Muslims of Valencia in the Age of Fernando and Isabel: Between Coexistence and Crusade* (University of California Press, 1991) - a wide-ranging survey of religious and social attitudes in Valencia.

7 Foreign Affairs

C.R. Boxer, *The Church Militant and Iberian Expansion, 1440-1770* (Baltimore, 1978) - assesses the role of the Church in Spain's colonial activities.

G. Mattingly, *Renaissance Diplomacy* (Penguin, 1965) - a pioneering (and still useful) review of international diplomacy in the early modern period.

R.B. Merriman, *The Rise of the Spanish Empire in the Old World and in the New,* 4 vols. (New York, 1918, repr. 1962) - regarded as a classic account but most modern students will find it very heavy reading.

A. Pagden, *Spanish Imperialism and the Political Imagination* (New Haven, 1989) - an interesting explanation of the origins and development of imperial ideas and activities in fifteenth-century Spain. Principally for the specialist.

8 Source Materials

G.A. Bergenroth (ed), *Calendar of Letters, Despatches and State Papers Relating to the Negotiations between England and Spain, Preserved in the Archives at Simancas and Elsewhere, 1485-1509* (London, 1862).

Andrés Bernáldez, *Memorias del Reinado de los Reyes Católicos,* ed. M. Gomez-Moreno and Juan de M. Carriazo (Blass SA, Madrid, 1962).

Andrés Bernáldez, *Historia de los reyes católicos D. Fernando y D. Isabel* vol. 2 (Seville, 1870).

N. Machiavelli, *The Prince,* ed. G. Bull (Penguin, 1981).

F. del Pulgar, *Crónica de los Reyes Católicos,* ed Juan de Mata Carriazo, 2 vols. (Madrid, 1943).

F. del Pulgar, *Letras, Glosa a las coplas de Mingo Revulgo,* ed. J. Dominguez Bordona (Madrid, 1929).

Glossary

Alcabala	a 10 per cent sales tax
Alcalde	a magistrate
Alcázar	a citadel or fortress
Aljamas	a walled area or ghetto in a town which separated Jews and *Moriscos* from the Christians
Audiencia	a court of appeal
Auto de fe	a ceremony or 'act of faith' at which penitents were encouraged by the Inquisition to abjure their beliefs before receiving sentence
Bandos	bands or groups which took political sides and caused civil disturbances
Biga	the ruling group in Barcelona in 1462, characterised by their wealth and property
Busca	merchants and shopkeepers in Barcelona who challenged the Biga for political power
Cañadas	royal sheepwalks
Casa de Contratación	a House of Trade in Seville which controlled all vessels, commerce and passengers travelling between Castile and America
Confraternity	a brotherhood which safeguarded the working and spiritual welfare of its members
Consulado	a board of directors responsible for controlling a town's trade
Conversos	Jews who were converted to Christianity
Convivencia	coexistence of Christianity, Islam and Judaism
Corregidores	Crown governors appointed to Castilian towns
Cortes	representative assembly in each kingdom (known as Corts in Catalonia)
Cruzada	Papal subsidy to help fund the war against Granada
Diputación	Aragonese committee that met in the absence of the Cortes
Encomienda	a grant of land from the Crown
Fueros	Aragonese laws and privileges
Hermandades	Castilian brotherhoods which kept order in the countryside
Hidalguía	lowest level of noble status exempt from taxation
Juros	credit bonds paid annually to the Crown bankers out of state revenue
Justiciar	Aragonese law officer in charge of courts and justice

Letrado	lawyer usually with two academic degrees and ten years' legal experience
Mayorazgo	entail confining the inheritance of an estate to one person
Mercedes	a royal grant or gift
Mesta	sheep owners' guild established to control the royal sheepwalks
Military orders	medieval crusading orders of Santiago, Calatrava and Alcántara
Monarquía	the dominions of the Spanish crowns
Morisco	a Christianized Muslim
Mudéjar	a Muslim living under Christian rule
Pactos	an agreement by which the Crown in Aragon agreed to uphold the *fueros*
Partidas	a legal code established by Alfonso X which became the basis of Castilian law
Pragmática	a royal decree
Procuradores	delegates elected to the Castilian Cortes
Reconquista	the 'Reconquest', by which the Moors were expelled from Spain
Regidores	town councillors
Remensa	a payment in Catalonia by which a serf gained his freedom
Residencia	an enquiry or audit into the conduct of a royal official
Señorío	a lordship or sovereignty over an area of land or community
Servicio	a 'service' or grant of taxation by the Cortes
Sometent	Valencian rural police force similar to the Hermandad
Suprema	royal council established in 1483 to supervise all Spanish inquisitions
Tása	a tax designed to control the price of goods
Tercia real	Church tithes payable to the Crown

N.B. For simplicity native terms and place-names have been given in Castilian, with occasional exceptions where familiarity to students dictated otherwise. Proper names, however, have been given in English. Thus, Isabella has been preferred to Isabel, Ferdinand to Fernando, and Joanna to Juana. Spanish terms (e.g. *corregidores*, *alcabala*) have been italicised throughout. Money in the fifteenth century was reckoned in *maravedís* in Castile and in *libras* in Aragon; and from 1497, the main gold coin was the ducat and the main silver coin the real in all Hispanic kingdoms.

Index

Aguilar, Alonso de 25, 44, 48
alcabala 4, 41, 44, 118
Alcaçovas, treaty of 27, 93-4
Alexander VI 71-2, 84, 97, 99, 106
Alfonso V, King of Portugal 19, 26-7, 30-1, 93

Beltrán de la Cueva 5, 28, 41
Bernáldez, Andrés 28-9, 47, 73, 75, 105

Casa de Contratación 60, 63, 66, 115
Charles V 45-6, 71, 78, 108, 110-11
Charles VIII 98-9
Cisneros, Cardinal and Archbishop 45-6, 70-1, 80, 82-3, 85, 93, 97, 111
cloth trade 6, 58, 60, 62-6
colonisation 94-7, 108
Columbus, Christopher 56, 95-6
corregidor 4, 11, 25, 30, 37-9, 47, 110
Cortes 3, 10-13, 27, 36-8, 40, 41, 44, 54, 74
councils, royal 3, 4, 35, 48
cruzada 44, 72, 79-80, 115

Diputación 10-12, 27, 36, 115

economy 5-6, 11-12, 57-66, 107-8, 110
Enríquez family 4, 6, 13, 20, 23, 41, 48

Fajardo family 4, 7, 41-2
foreign affairs 9-10, 13-15, 89-102

González de Mendoza, Pedro 5, 21, 23-4, 57, 70, 73

Henry IV, King of Castile 1-8, 15, 19, 22, 26, 28-31, 41, 47, 61
Henry VII, King of England 49, 65, 98, 101
Henry VIII, King of England 99-101
Hermandad 3, 25-6, 30, 35-6, 38-40, 42, 44, 79, 110, 115
hidalguía 6, 23, 42
Holy League 92, 99-100
humanism 9, 14, 64, 71

Inquisition 35, 38, 64, 72-8, 81-5, 105, 107-8, 110, 116
Isabella, Queen of Castile 2, 5, 13, 19-31, 34-49, 53-6, 58-66,
69-85, 89-102, 104-11

Jews 8, 9, 14, 64, 66, 72-8, 82, 84-5, 105
Joanna 'la Beltráneja' 4-5, 21-31
Joanna, Queen of Castile 45, 99, 108, 110
John II, King of Aragon 1, 10, 13, 15, 19, 27, 100
juros 44, 79, 107, 115

Lemos, Count of 42, 46-7
letrados 35, 54, 116
Louis XI 13, 26-7, 49, 65
Louis XII 95, 100

Machiavelli, Niccolò 90, 92, 101-2, 105
Manrique, Gómez 15, 41, 47, 105
Maximilian I 46, 99-101
Mendoza family 4, 7, 21, 41, 45, 48, 55, 80
mercedes 23, 43, 116
Mesta 6, 58-9, 65, 116
Muslims 6-8, 14, 40, 66, 69, 72, 98

Nájera, Duke of 42, 46-7

Papacy 21, 27, 31, 43, 69, 71-5, 84, 90, 99, 106
patronage 23, 44, 53-4, 72, 105
Philip the Fair, Archduke of Flanders 45, 48, 99, 108
plague 5, 12, 56, 59
Portugal, Crown of 1, 9-10, 27, 89, 93-7, 101
Pulgar, Fernando del 25-6, 28-31, 46-7, 73, 75, 79, 105

Reconquest 7-8, 14, 78-80, 94, 105, 108, 116

shipbuilding 6, 58, 63, 66
slaves 56, 94, 96-7, 101

taxation 3-4, 6, 24, 43-4, 65, 72, 79
Tendilla, Count of 36, 41-2, 45, 54, 80-1
Torquemada, Tomás de 74-6, 85, 105

Valera, Diego de 28, 46, 104-5
Velasco family 23, 39, 46-8
Villena, Marquis of 4, 5, 22-4, 30, 41-2, 45-6, 55